Presenting T/
Current Worldwide Healing Movement

Healing For Everyone
Volume 1:
Four Kinds Of People
by Curry R. Blake

General Overseer

John G. Lake Ministries

and

Dominion Life

International Apostolic Church

Copyright © 2016 by Curry R. Blake
All Rights Reserved

Published by
CHRISTIAN REALITY BOOKS
P.O. Box 742947
Dallas TX 75374
1-888-293-6591

Unless otherwise noted, all Scripture quotations are taken from the King James Bible.

The Names:
Divine Healing Technician(s)
John G. Lake Ministries
John G. Lake Healing Rooms
John G. Lake's Divine Healing Institute
and all derivatives of these names are copyrighted trademarks and may not be used without the express written permission of
John G. Lake Ministries
P. O. Box 742947
Dallas, Texas 75374
www.jglm.org

Please advise us if you come into contact with anyone using the names:
John G. Lake
John G. Lake Ministries
John G. Lake's Divine Healing Institute
John G. Lake Healing Rooms
Divine Healing Technicians
Certified DHT

This book or parts thereof may not be reproduced in any form without express written permission of Curry Blake.

Printed in the United States of America.

Endorsements

"Because of your fulfillment of my father's prophecy concerning his successor and the fact that you pursued the truth about healing and never once asked about how to get his anointing, we knew you were the person to carry on the ministry like my father."
       Gertrude and Wilford Reidt
    John G. Lake's daughter and son-in-law

"Curry is obviously the man chosen by God to carry the mantle of John G. Lake. The proof is in the results of his ministry. He will change the face of Christianity in America and anywhere his message is received."
              Sid Roth
     "Messianic Vision" Radio Talk Show Host

"Curry is a reproducer of reproducers that reproduce reproducers. As an apostle he walks in an authority and power that is seldom seen, yet he is able to remain humble, touchable, and reachable."
          Bishop Bill Hamon
      Christian International Ministries

"Curry's message is scripturally accurate and theologically flawless."
          Dr. Michael L. Brown
  F.I.R.E. School of Ministry Pensacola Revival

"We work with Bro. Curry because what he does works!"

David Hogan
Missionary - Freedom Ministries

"While there are many who claim Lake as their spiritual inspiration, Curry Blake's success in the healing ministry and his vision of Christianity are uniquely reminiscent of Lake himself."

Robert Liardon
Author of *God's Generals*; Pentecostal Historian

TABLE OF CONTENTS

FOREWARD 1
INTRODUCTION 3
HEALING FOR EVERYONE VOLUME 1: FOUR KINDS OF PEOPLE 9
CHAPTER 1: HEALING FOR THE WORLD (THE UNSAVED) 11
CHAPTER 2: HEALING FOR THE BRAND NEW CHRISTIAN 17
CHAPTER 3: HEALING FOR THE CARNAL CHRISTIAN 24
CHAPTER 4: HEALING FOR THE SPIRITUAL CHRISTIAN 43
CHAPTER 5: WHOSE FAITH? 62
QUESTIONS AND ANSWERS ABOUT HEALING 66
CERTIFIED DIVINE HEALING'TECHNICIAN (DHT) STATUS 90
WHAT THE BIBLE SAYS ABOUT DIVINE HEALING 92
CURRY R. BLAKE (JGLM) BASIC PRINCIPLES 94
THE HISTORY OF JOHN G. LAKE HEALING ROOMS 96
PROPHETIC WORD GIVEN BY JOHN G. LAKE 99
THURSDAY, MAY 24, 1934 – SPOKANE, WA. 99
JOHN G. LAKE'S LETTER TO'CARRIE JUDD MONTGOMERY . 101
HOW TO ENTER THE WILL OF GOD BY: JOHN G. LAKE 105
PROPHECY TO CURRY BLAKE BY BISHOP BILL HAMON 107
PROPHETIC WORD TO CURRY BLAKE'THROUGH BILL HAMON 124
PROPHETIC WORD SPOKEN BY SIMEON STEWART TO CURRY BLAKE 130

PROPHETIC WORD GIVEN THROUGH SIMEON STEWART TO CURRY R. BLAKE 132

JOHN G. LAKE MINISTRIES 145
   A: THE INTERNATIONAL DIVINE HEALING ASSOCIATION: 145
   B: THE INTERNATIONAL APOSTOLIC COUNCIL: 145
   C: ORDINATION AND/OR LICENSING: 146
   D: CHURCH PLANTING: 147
   E: LIFETEAMS: 147
   F: DIVINE HEALING INSTITUTE: 148
   G: IABC/JGLSOM – DOMINION BIBLE INSTITUTE: 149
   H: DOMINION LIFE MOVEMENT: 150
   J: JGLM PARTNER PROGRAM: 150

Foreword

For some time now, the Spirit of God has been dealing with me about separating myself in a secluded place and writing out the detailed principles and truths that have helped so many people around the world to launch out into ministering the life and power of Jesus to a sick and hurting world.

One such period of time has led to this book.

As I was writing it, I knew that this was to be the first of a series of books along this line. I believe it is important that the details, the nuggets that I have learned over the last 40-plus years of studying and ministering healing, be written down and published so that others may learn and continue growing in the path to minister like Jesus.

A lot of the nuggets herein have been learned at the cost of someone's life.

As I often say, we analyze our failures, not our victories. As we analyze the failures—which, by the way, means that someone died because we did not know what we needed to know to get them healed—we discover biblical truths that lead to victory the next time.

I realize that a lot of what I teach and will say in these books will be the exact opposite of what is currently taught concerning healing. I can't help that. I simply write and teach what God points out to me in Scripture.

As I sit in a hotel room in Melbourne, Florida, writing this, I can say that I have been especially conscious of God bringing out specific things that He wanted included. I can also say that I especially like writing, because I am also very conscious of the fact that I learn something new every time I sit down to write.

I know that even writing a foreword like this is unusual, but then I've never shied away from doing things differently.

I hope this book blesses you and that you come to a knowledge of the Truth and walk in it.

If I can be of any help in your development, feel free to contact me.

Blessings,
Curry R. Blake

Introduction

Every book should have a "why." Why another book? The why of this book is simple.

I wrote this book so that you could have the simple truths of divine healing.

These are the truths that have birthed the current street healing movement and the truths that have launched thousands of everyday believers (just like you) into full-time ministry. EVERY person seen as a leader in the current street healing movement was either taught personally by me or by watching the Divine Healing Technician Training by video.

Hundreds of thousands have already been healed and delivered just by believers putting these truths into action.

Lives have been changed. Eyes once blind now see!
People once in wheelchairs can now walk and run.
Their lives have been given back to them. Even the dead have been raised! (For testimonies, feel free to visit our website: www.jglm.org)

I could have kept this information secret or used it to become rich or famous. Instead, I decided to share it openly with anyone who would listen. Why? Because I have a grave where my daughter is buried just south of McKinney, Texas.

Had I known then what I know now, she would still be alive. But I didn't know it then. Her death actually drove me to search until I found the truth.

When I stood by her little white casket on February 14, 1981, I made a vow to God: "Father, there was no man there for me when I needed one. But if You will teach me the truth about divine healing, I will be that man for someone else, so that they will not have a grave like I do now."

That event started my quest for truth, and the material in this book is what I found. From that moment on, I began to study everything I could find concerning divine healing and the power of God.

I went to every conference I could find. I even quit jobs when I could not get the time off, just so I could attend a camp meeting or conference where I heard that they were going to be teaching on healing, or if I heard that someone who'd had success in healing was going to be there.

Introduction

I heard of such names as Smith Wigglesworth, Aimee Semple McPherson, A. A. Allen, Jack Coe, John Alexander Dowie, John G. Lake, and many more. I heard of their great exploits and the many miracles, but then I ran into a problem; they were all dead!

I could read their books and their life stories but beyond that, they couldn't help me. But I noticed that there was something different about John Lake. He not only had many healings and miracles occur under his own hands, he also trained others to minister healing, and they achieved the same results.

When I saw that, I knew I had found my mentor. Unfortunately, he was already dead also. So my next step was to find his relatives and contact them, just as I had contacted Smith Wigglesworth's family and the families and friends of all the others. I had even moved my entire family to South Bend, Indiana, just so I could learn from Dr. Lester Sumrall. He became my mentor, my Bible teacher, and my pastor. I often say that I was taught faith in Tulsa, but I learned faith in South Bend.

As I conversed weekly (for a 7-year period) with John Lake's daughter and son-in-law, I asked questions and received the answers I needed. Toward the end of our relationship (Gertrude died, and Wilford would not last much longer) I was given box after box of letters, prophetic words, sermons, and notes of John G. Lake's that had been preserved by Gertrude and Wilford, and from several other family members and friends of the family, along with a list of names of over 100 people who had been members of John Lake's last church in Spokane, Washington.

Many of them had known Divine Healing Technicians that John Lake himself had trained. Again I asked each of them question after question. Finally, in April of 1995, while on a trip to Houston, Texas, to hear Pauline Parham (daughter-in-law of Charles F. Parham, the founder of the Pentecostal Movement) preach, I found a person on the list of names who was in a Houston, Texas, senior care facility. Her name was Jennie Jeters. I visited her and began asking the same questions.

Finally, she became wearied with my questions and told me that I merely needed to read the DHT manual Dr. Lake used to teach the DHT, and my questions would be answered. I agreed, but said I didn't know where I could find one. She said she had one and that I could read it but couldn't have it until she died. Two years later, I received the manual. It changed everything!

Literally, everything I had been taught was clearly wrong. I noticed that many of the sermons had the same names that I had seen before, but there were differences.

Introduction

Then I found out that many of the sermons that had already been published had been edited. Most of them, drastically edited. As I read the unedited sermons, I realized why they had been edited. If they had been left untouched, the material in them would have refuted everything then being taught about healing.

I saw that the Church had become so afraid of being sued or persecuted that they had backed off of the very teaching that brought the power of God as witness. I realized why we seldom saw miracles in healing services, and I decided to do something about it.

I first began practicing everything I was learning in my home, at the local Walmart, restaurants, and grocery stores. Everywhere I went, it worked.

It didn't matter if the person was a Christian or not, or if they had faith or not. For nine months in my home, EVERY person who came there for healing received healing. Sometimes it took a few weeks, but every person was healed.

Then I decided I could not keep it to myself, I had to teach it to others. A friend put together a quick website and put my phone number on. It said if anyone needed healing, they should call me.

Within a couple of hours, I received a call from North Carolina. I traveled there with my daughter and ministered for a week in three homes each day. I ministered to over 200 people, 40 of whom had cancer. At the end of the week everyone was healed, including the 40 cancer victims.

Sid Roth heard about the results we were having and invited me to be a guest on his radio and television program. Since that day, I have never had to look for or ask for a place to minister. We are consistently scheduled as much as I want to be.

The material in this book will change your life. It is simple, but quite simply, it is also the most effective teaching on divine healing in existence, because it is simply all BIBLE!

Read it, study it, DO IT!

Curry R. Blake
August 24, 2016

Healing For Everyone
Volume 1: Four Kinds Of People

Healing Provided for Anyone at Any Level of Spiritual Development

Any time you attempt to teach a subject that deals with the heart of God (which is any time you teach about anything that deals with God or His willingness to get involved in the lives of humans), you either have to go into a long dissertation concerning theological terminology and principles of biblical interpretation or you simply assume your reader will have already reached a level of spiritual maturity and understanding that allows them to believe that God is good and that He wants to become involved in the affairs of men's lives.

In this book, I am making that assumption, along with others, such as:

A. God still heals.

B. Physical healing is included in Jesus' sacrificial death. (If you need assurance in that area I suggest you read T. J. McCrossan's book, *Bodily Healing and the Atonement*.)

C. God wants to use YOU to set the captives free through divine healing.

If those assumptions concerning you are correct, then we can get started.

Chapter 1
Healing for The World (The Unsaved)

Mark 16:14–20

14 Afterward he appeared unto the eleven as they sat at meat, and upbraided them with their unbelief and hardness of heart, because they believed not them which had seen him after he was risen.

In this verse, Jesus appears to the disciples while they are eating. They have already had several eyewitnesses tell them that they have seen Jesus with their own eyes and that He has risen, just as He said He would, and yet they still do not believe. He immediately scolds them and rebukes them for not believing.

15 And he said unto them, Go ye into all the world, and preach the gospel to every creature.

Here Jesus commands them to go into all the world preaching the gospel, the good news of Jesus' resurrection and of the Kingdom of God. They are to preach (proclaim with an authority and solemnity that what they say must be listened to and obeyed!) to everyone. They are not to pick and choose whom they preach the gospel to.

Note: Jesus NEVER commissioned anyone to preach the gospel without telling them to also heal the sick.

Healing the sick is an actual part of the "preaching" (proclaiming) of the good news.

16 He that believeth and is baptized shall be saved; but he that believeth not shall be damned.

Just to be clear, we need to recognize here that the "he that believeth" in verse 16 is a person the disciples are going to go into all the world to preach to. The "he that believeth" is not referring to one of the eleven disciples. So follow closely as we find out what this new believer, the one whom is preached to and believes and is saved can do:.

17 And these signs shall follow them that believe; In my name shall they cast out devils; they shall speak with new tongues;

"These signs." Notice the plurality of signs mentioned here. There are several signs that are to follow this new believer.

18 They shall take up serpents; and if they drink any deadly thing, it shall not hurt them; they shall lay hands on the sick, and they shall recover.

One of the signs is that they will lay hands on the sick and the sick shall recover. There are several things to take note of here.

First, it says that they will do these signs "in my Name," meaning, in the Name of Jesus. But notice it DOES NOT say that they will lay hands on the sick AND PRAY.

It simply says that in His Name, believers (new believers) will lay hands on the sick and they (the sick unbeliever) will be healed.

There are two major points here.

1. There are no words needed, so you don't have to worry about "praying wrong."

As a matter of fact, we could even say that IF you pray, you've already prayed wrong. I'm not saying that if you pray you are doing wrong and the person won't get healed. I am simply emphasizing that you do not have to pray. You can simply lay your hands on a sick UNBELIEVER and expect them to get well because you are doing it in Jesus' name (which also means: 'in His stead"). You are doing it in His stead because Jesus is not technically there in the flesh to do it Himself.

It is always good to say, "In the Name of Jesus, BE HEALED!"

2. Since this aspect of healing is to be a sign to the unbeliever who is having the gospel preached to them, it is obvious that they are not expected to have faith for their healing. Otherwise, they would not need a sign of healing to become a believer.

We can see from this that God has made a way for unbelievers to be healed.

The method is simple.

Believers preach the gospel to unbelievers and then the believer lays hands on the unbeliever in the Name of Jesus, allowing the life of God to flow into the unbeliever, which heals the unbeliever. When the unbeliever is healed, it should be a natural course of events that they submit their lives to the Lordship of Jesus.

19 So then after the Lord had spoken unto them, he was received up into heaven, and sat on the right hand of God.
20 And they went forth, and preached everywhere, the Lord working with them, and confirming the word with signs following. Amen.

Notice here that they went everywhere preaching the gospel. As they went, the Lord worked with and confirmed the word of God that was preached.

Now the natural question would be:
Whose faith got them healed? We know it was not the faith of the unbeliever. They were unbelievers.

We also know that many times people were healed under Jesus' ministry who did not have faith.

The man who brought his son to Jesus in Matthew 17 admitted he had unbelief. We know he didn't have faith for his son's healing or his son would have been healed already.

We know that it was a lack of faith that kept the boy from being healed by the disciples because Jesus told them that their failure to get the boy healed was due to their unbelief, which is exactly what the boy's father said he had.

So we know that it was Jesus' faith that healed the boy. We know that when Jesus raised the widow of Nain's son from the dead, no one there had faith except Jesus. The son was dead (obviously, no faith being used), the widow was crying (obviously, no faith being used).

When the centurion's servant was healed in Matthew 8, there is no evidence of anyone using faith except the centurion. So it is obvious that the centurion was having faith for someone else. There are many examples of this principle throughout Scripture.

As a further point to contemplate…if you cannot have faith for another person, then all intercession is useless. No one should ever be allowed to stand in proxy for another person. (We will look at this more in depth later on.)

I suggest you complete the Divine Healing Technician Training to further study these principles.

So in Mark 16, it shows God has made healing available to the unsaved when a believer will exercise faith and use Kingdom dominion.

Chapter 2
Healing For The Brand-New Christian

James 5:14-15
14 Is any sick among you? Let him call for the elders of the church; and let them pray over him, anointing him with oil in the name of the Lord:
15 And the prayer of faith shall save the sick, and the Lord shall raise him up; and if he have committed sins, they shall be forgiven him.

In this section, we will look at how God has even made healing available to the newest Christian believer. This person is such a new believer that he doesn't even know what he doesn't know.

The Book of James was the first book written of the New Testament. It was written as a primer to teach new believers how to live the Christian life. Everything you need to know concerning the basic Christian life is included in the Book of James. For example, how to treat people who are not as fortunate as you.

You must watch your words and how powerful and dangerous your tongue can be. You are told how to deal with strained relationships. New believers are also instructed on what to do if they get sick.
There are several things to notice in this short passage.

1. Verse 14 starts off by saying, "Is any sick among you?"

In any modern church there would be no need to ask if there were any sick among the members, because practically every church has sick people in its midst.

2. Verse 14 goes on to say that the sick person(s) should call for the elders of the church. This verse, along with verse 15, tells us the exact process the sick one, ANY sick one, ALL sick ones in any church, are to take to get well. They are to call for the Elders of the church.

Every sick person in any church is commanded, according to James 5:14–15, to call for the Elders of the church, with the expected result being that they will come to the sick person. Notice, the sick person is not told to go to the elders or to get in line at the next church service. It says they are to call the elders and the elders will go to them and anoint them with oil and pray the prayer of faith over the sick one and THE PRAYER OF FAITH SHALL SAVE (heal and deliver) the sick and The Lord SHALL raise him up.

Pay particular attention to the next part.

"…and if he has committed sins, they will be forgiven him."

Do you see it?

The first point here is that the elders are to go and pray the prayer of faith. That means that for someone to be an Elder, they have to know how to pray the prayer of faith that can get the sick healed.

The second point is that the sick person only had to call for the elders. There is nothing in this verse about the sick person having faith to be healed. If the sick person had faith to be healed, they wouldn't need the Elders to pray the prayer of faith for them, they could pray it for themselves.

The third point is that the prayer of faith (prayed by an Elder) was expected to bring healing to any sick person who asked them to pray.

Notice how there was no question as to the Lord's will in the matter. It was expected that the Elder, and even the sick person, would know that it was always God's will to heal anyone, anytime, regardless of the cause.

The next point is one of particular importance, especially in this day and time. It destroys one of the most pervasive doctrines of devils currently accepted by the overall Body of Christ…

The last half of verse 15 says plainly: "and IF he has committed sins, they SHALL be forgiven him."

The first thing to notice here is that it says "IF" the sick person has committed sins they shall be forgiven.

This points out the fact that every sickness is not caused by a person committing a particular sin. If every sickness were caused by sin, then the word "if" would not have been used.

So, any doctrine or practice that teaches us to automatically associate particular sins to a specific disease as a punishment is automatically wrong.

Please note here that I am not saying that particular sins won't bring particular diseases. In many cases, there can be a direct correlation. For example, promiscuity can bring specific sexually transmitted diseases. There would be a direct transmission of disease from one person to another.

That is not God punishing the sinner with a disease, it is simply sowing and reaping. But as it states in this verse, all sickness is not the result of sin. In some cases, people become sick by sowing and reaping. In other cases, they may simply be under a direct attack from satan and not know how to stand against the attack. Another possible cause is what is known as retaliation. When you start to inflict damage to satan and his works, he will often turn his attention onto you and retaliate. This is often when you have been interceding in a situation for which satan is to blame.

What I am referring to here, for example, is the common practice of automatically declaring that a person has bitterness if they are diagnosed as having arthritis. This is commonly referred to as the "spiritual roots of diseases."

There are several things wrong with that teaching and practice. I will give you two reasons you should not participate in this practice.

1) JESUS NEVER DID IT!

2) The moment you do it, you change your position from one as a deliverer to one as a judge.

Remember this:

The only person who has to know how the problem started is someone who does not have the power to set one free!

When you have the power to set the person free, you don't look for how they became a captive, you simply set them free and begin discipling them to become followers of Jesus.

The final point I will make here concerning James 5:14–15 is this: The verses say, "Is ANY SICK among you…" ANY SICK! This is the same language used for salvation. Any, whosoever, etc.

This is not a single, specific case that James personally knew about and knew that it was God's will to heal in this case, but maybe not in other cases.

It says, ANY SICK.

This is the way for ANY SICK person who is part of a fellowship of Christians that has Elders in it to be healed. This is a general statement to any sick person.

These verses prove that it is ALWAYS God's desire and will to heal ANY SICK PERSON. All they have to do is find a person who can pray the prayer of faith. Hopefully (and scripturally), any elder in any fellowship of Christians should know how to pray the prayer of faith that can get the sick healed.

In the church I pastor in Plano (North Dallas), Texas, we do not allow any person to be considered or placed into position as an elder unless they have been proven to be able to get the sick healed. Part of this process is that they must become Certified Divine Healing Technicians. (For more information on becoming a CDHT, please contact us at www.jglm.org)

You can see from all that I've said so far that God has made provision for both the unsaved and the newly saved to be healed from any sickness. All God has to do is find a Christian who will lay hands on the sick and/or pray the prayer of faith.

Our specialty at John G. Lake Ministries is doing exactly that!

Chapter 3
Healing For The Carnal Christian

The next area of providing healing for everyone in the world at any phase of spiritual development can be seen in 1 Corinthians 11:23–32.

Before we delve into 1 Corinthians 11, let's first look at 1 Corinthians 3.

I know this is a lot of Scripture, but it is important that you see what Paul was saying to the Corinthians in 1 Corinthians 3 before we point out the impact of it in 1 Corinthians 11.

When Paul began writing his letter to the Corinthians, he stated that they were carnal.

1 Corinthians 3:1–4
1 And I, brethren, could not speak unto you as unto spiritual, but as unto carnal, even as unto babes in Christ.

Paul tells the Corinthians that they are so carnal that he cannot speak to them as spiritual, but only as babies in Christ, which he characterizes as "carnal."

The word "carnal" means, "flesh oriented" or "directed by the feelings of the soul and/or body." It means to let your feelings (emotions and/or the physical body) dictate how you act, speak, and live. It means to be more oriented toward the physical realm than the spiritual realm.

The vast majority of "Christians" are carnally minded. Even believers who have been born again for many, many years can remain carnally minded and not grow up spiritually. Bible knowledge does not determine spiritual growth.

Most carnal Christians have a lot of knowledge of the Bible Scriptures. They can quote Scripture and spout the right doctrines to fit in with their group because they would more accurately be called "indoctrinated" rather than spiritual.

The best way to determine whether a person is carnal or spiritual is to look at the fruit of their lives. If their lives match their speech and their speech lines up with the word of God, then they are usually spiritual and have grown out of carnality.

If their lives are still encumbered with the affairs of the world, and if they are still struggling with habits and addictions that they had before they became born again, they are still carnally minded. (The church must begin to again emphasize making Jesus the Lord of His followers rather than just repeating a prayer and shaking a preacher's hand.)

2 I have fed you with milk, and not with meat: for hitherto ye were not able to bear it, neither yet now are ye able.
3 For ye are yet carnal: for whereas there is among you envying, and strife, and divisions, are ye not carnal, and walk as men?

In this verse, Paul gives a basic test between carnality and spirituality. If you engage in envy, strife, and divisions, you are carnal!

4 For while one saith, I am of Paul; and another, I am of Apollos; are ye not carnal?

Paul emphasizes that spiritual believers look past the messenger and realize that if the message is accurate, it is God speaking through His messenger. This should remind us to stay away from Christian idolatry and putting one minister on a higher pedestal than another. It should also remind ministers to constantly climb down off the pedestal they frequently get put on.

This passage shows that the Corinthians were carnal and that when Paul wrote the entire letter (including chapters 11 and 12), he was talking to carnal believers.

That's right; the gifts mentioned in chapter 12 were experiences the Corinthians were already having. Paul was simply explaining what they were experiencing, and Paul even said that even though they were carnal, they were having experiences many other more spiritual Christians weren't having.

The gifts aren't given because someone attains a heightened level of spirituality. They are given because carnal Christians need help and don't know how to have their needs met by faith and the fullness of the Spirit, so God has to help them by manifesting Himself in a Word of Knowledge or a Gift of Healing.

Gifts simply mean you're available. Fruit means you are faithful. Gifts are given instantly, while fruit grows over time.

Now that we've proven that the Corinthians were carnal, let's look at how God has provided for them to be healed.

From all accounts, The Lord's Table, commonly known as Communion, was practiced on a regular basis. Very likely it was even practiced on a daily basis by the early church. (For more on Communion, please read my booklet entitled, *Communion*.)

Now let's look at how the everyday, average carnal believer can be healed.

First, let me ask you a simple question.

When and how often can you partake in communion? If your answer is, "Any time I want to," or "Every day, if I wanted to," remember that as we look at the Scriptures.

1 Corinthians 11:23–32

23 For I have received of the Lord that which also I delivered unto you, That the Lord Jesus the same night in which he was betrayed took bread:

Paul received this by revelation from Jesus Himself.

24 And when he had given thanks, he brake it, and said, Take, eat: this is my body, which is broken for you: this do in remembrance of me.

Notice that Jesus referred to the communion bread as "my body, which was broken for you." He said to eat the bread in remembrance of Him. We will see momentarily that He also warned us to make sure we know what we are remembering and why we are eating the bread.

In some cases, we have been told that the bread represents the Church (which is also referred to as "His body." He was NOT referring to the Church when He referred to His body here, because the church has never been broken for any individual member of the body of Christ.

What He was referring to here as His body was His actual physical body, which was broken for each one of us at the whipping post where He received the Roman scourging.

As an important side point here, let me remind everyone that Jesus DID NOT receive 39 stripes! The 39 stripes rule (40 stripes minus 1) was a Jewish law, NOT a Roman law. Jesus was whipped under Roman Law, NOT Jewish law. When Jesus was whipped, he received as many lashes as the Roman scourger desired. He was whipped with a "flagellum," which was similar to a cat-of-nine-tails with pieces of metal, bone, and glass in the ends, which were intended to rip the flesh to shreds.

The actual Hebrew word used to prophetically describe the event in Isaiah 53:5 is *chabbuwrah*.

Strong's Concordance: OT: 2250 chabbuwrah (khab-boo-raw'); or chabburah (khab-boo-raw'); or chaburah (khaboo-raw'); from OT: 2266; properly, bound (with stripes), i.e. a weal (or black-and-blue mark itself): KJV - blueness, bruise, hurt, stripe, wound.

The important thing here is that the word used was in the singular meaning that it should be translated as: by his "stripe." What that signifies is that Jesus received so many whippings that there was not a single quarter-inch of his skin that wasn't ripped, torn, or bruised. If there had been a single area of one quarter-inch that was not touched, then the accuracy of God's word would have required the word to have been in the plural rather than the singular.

That's how trustworthy God's Word is! Every mark made on His body was for OUR healing.

Another point I want to make here is that there are NOT 39 categories of disease.

I know it sounds cool to say that Jesus received 39 stripes and that there are 39 categories of disease, but it just isn't true! If we do not make sure that we are accurate in our presentation of God's wonderful salvation, we cannot expect God to endorse or confirm what we are saying.

Also, if someone listening to you hears you say that and knows it isn't true (like a doctor), he may speak up and embarrass you, or worse, he may not get saved because of your inaccuracies.

The eating of the bread represents you receiving the benefits of that whipping; the whipping that provided your physical healing from sickness and disease.

Many churches do not believe in physical healing through Jesus' atonement. They do not know why they should eat the bread of communion. They know why they should drink the cup. They know the cup represents the blood Jesus shed for the remission of sins. But they do not believe in the stripes, nor the benefits they provide.

25 After the same manner also he took the cup, when he had supped, saying, This cup is the new testament in my blood: this do ye, as oft as ye drink it, in remembrance of me.
26 For as often as ye eat this bread, and drink this cup, ye do shew the Lord's death till he come.
27 Wherefore whosoever shall eat this bread, and drink this cup of the Lord, unworthily, shall be guilty of the body and blood of the Lord.

This verse is the part of the key to understanding this section of 1 Corinthians. The word "unworthily" used here means to eat or drink the elements of the Lord's Table in an irreverent or flippant manner, not taking into account the seriousness of the sacrifice and understanding the value of the benefit provided by that sacrifice. It tells us that if we partake of the Lord's Table without giving the bread and the juice its due recognition, then we will be guilty of doing so and will incur a due penalty.

Most people give the juice due recognition. It represents the blood of Jesus that was poured out to redeem us. Most would not be "guilty of the blood" in that respect, but many within Bible-believing churches are "guilty of the body" because they simply eat the bread without focusing on the fact that it represents the body that bore the stripes that paid for our physical bodily healing.

If those who believe in divine healing are guilty of not giving the bread/body its due recognition, how much more would those who do not believe in divine healing be guilty by eating the bread without focusing on the value of the sacrifice Jesus paid? The following verses prove this.

28 But let a man examine himself, and so let him eat of that bread, and drink of that cup.

Here, the Apostle Paul tells us what to do as we partake of the Lord's Table. We are to examine ourselves to make sure we are not guilty of the body and the blood.

We are to focus on the value of the sacrifice Jesus provided. We do that by looking at and believing what the Bible says regarding that sacrifice.

In Isaiah 53:5 it says plainly that "with His stripes we are healed." This is also reiterated in 1 Peter 2:24 and Isaiah 53:5, and is connected to physical healing in Matthew 8:16–17. (For more in-depth study on "Healing In the Atonement" see my book on "Communion" or "The Divine Healing Technician Training.")

29 For he that eateth and drinketh unworthily, eateth and drinketh damnation to himself, not discerning the Lord's body.

Notice in this verse Paul switches from emphasis on "the blood" and points out that the person eating and drinking unworthily is not discerning the Lord's body.

As I stated earlier, every Christian understands, at least to some degree, the importance of the blood, but many if not most Christians do not understand the value of the body, referring to the stripes that the body bore.

What would be the result if the Lord's Table was not received properly (meaning with proper focus and understanding)?

The next verse tells us that very thing.

30 For this cause many are weak and sickly among you, and many sleep.

Paul says: "For this cause..." because some of the Corinthians (and also modern-day "Christians") do not partake of the Lord's Table properly...many are (physically) weak and (physically) sickly among you, and many sleep (die prematurely).

This is plainly stating that by partaking in Communion correctly, we can expect protection from getting sick, and if we are sick, we can be healed.

This verse is also referring to partaking of Communion with an expectation to living out our lives to their fullest length, simply by doing it right.

To further prove the connection between physical healing and "his stripes" and Communion, let us look at the present physical evidence as shown in the Church.

Today, in the churches that do not believe in divine healing at all, and in the churches that do believe in divine healing but do not connect the bread of the Communion Table to the stripes and broken body of Jesus, we can see that there is virtually no difference in the rates of sickness and premature death when compared to the statistics of the unbelieving world. But, if you compare the healing/health statistics of those churches that do believe in divine healing and practice the Lord's Table correctly, you will find that the statistics of healing/health and longevity far surpass those of the world.

The answer is simple: Do it right!'

31 For if we would judge ourselves, we should not be judged.

Look at this verse in light of the above statements. Every Christian needs to examine themselves when it comes to the Lord's Table and make sure that we are not just going through the motions. We need to judge ourselves to make sure we are holding that blood and those stripes in their proper place of esteem. If we do that, we can expect divine health and healing when we need it.

32 But when we are judged, we are chastened of the Lord, that we should not be condemned with the world.

In this verse, many have found fear and condemnation, when in reality it was meant to show us the care of our Heavenly Father. The problem comes if we have been wrongly taught the definition of "chastened of the Lord."

To quickly get a right understanding, let's start with the proper definition of "chasten" or "chastise." Many, if not most, Christians, have been taught that it means "to punish," which is one definition. But the full definition means "to train, instruct, to (instill) discipline."

We should recognize that if we discipline ourselves to value the benefits of the stripes, then we will not need to be instructed or trained by God to remember that Jesus bore the stripes for our healing. We will begin to automatically remember and partake of the Lord's Table with a right motive and remembrance. If we do so, we will be healed, if necessary, and stay healed (divine health).

I know this has been quite a long dissertation on this aspect of this topic, but I felt it necessary to give the details.

Now let's look at why it was necessary for me to add it in this section that is dealing with divine (physical) healing for the carnal Christian or the carnally minded Christian.

As we stated at the beginning of this section, the carnal-minded Christian is one who has become too focused on and dependent upon the physical realm. What that means is that they let their "flesh" (emotions, feelings, body, etc.) tell them how they feel or how to react to situations, rather than letting their spirit tell them how to react.

A person who constantly reacts to things or people in a way that is inconsistent with how Scripture tells us to react to things is a carnal-minded person.

For example:
A person (Christian) feels a pain or some other symptom. They go to a doctor, who runs tests and then tells them they have a particular illness or disease.

Immediately, that person is overwhelmed with fear that will also bring forth imaginations of dying, thoughts of how their children will make it without them, etc. If that fear leads to depression, that person is carnal-minded.

On the other hand, let's say the exact same scenario takes place, except instead of descending into depression, the person may have the same initial reaction where fear tries to get hold. But the spiritual-minded person "girds up the loins" of their mind and starts deciding on a plan of action. They do not capitulate their mind to the enemy, they begin doing spiritual warfare. They call any close spiritual friends they have and inform them concerning the situation. They mobilize a few close friends to begin speaking life and healing and commanding the disease to go. This will continue until they are completely healed and well.

The reason Communion is the most common way for a carnal person to get healed is because it allows them to have what Oral Roberts called a "point of contact." A point of contact is a physical thing, such as a cloth or specific time and day to set for their healing.

In Matthew 9, Mark 5 and Luke 8, we are given the testimony of the woman with an issue of blood. The woman set the time for her healing, and she set the physical point of contact that would allow her to receive her healing. She said that if she just touched the hem of Jesus' garment she would be healed.

Notice the word "touch." Carnal-minded people need to touch or feel something to set their time of healing. Carnality is not just in the feeling realm, it is also part of the faith mixture. Carnality is not just for a younger or newer believer. Carnality is a state in which anyone can be if they have not chosen to truly live by faith. It doesn't matter how long a person may have been a Christian.

A newborn Christian can decide to become spiritual-minded and do so, and a person who has been a Christian for forty years can still be carnally minded.

In Matthew 8:5–13, we see the story of the Centurion. He was a person who was not a part of the Abrahamic Covenant. Technically, he had no right to be healed by Jesus. When the Centurion told Jesus about his sick servant, Jesus immediately said He would go and heal him. (It even appears that Jesus interrupted the centurion, because the Centurion said that Jesus did not need to go to his house and physically touch the servant because he understood authority and knew that if Jesus gave a command, his servant would be healed.)

Notice here that the Centurion was operating in faith and did not need anything physical to place his faith upon. Jesus said the Centurion had more faith than anyone He had encountered up to that time. Notice the contrast between the Centurion and the woman with the issue of blood.

Matthew 9:21
*21 For she said within herself, <u>If I may but **touch** his garment</u>, I shall be whole.*

The woman placed her faith on touching; the Centurion placed his faith on the authority of Jesus' word.

These two stories are prime examples of the difference between a carnal mind using faith and a spiritual mind using faith.

The carnal mind always demands some type of physical touch or physical point of contact. But notice, even the carnally minded woman used faith and God met her where she was spiritually and healed her.

You do not have to attain some high, lofty spiritual peak to receive from God. God provided a way for even the carnally minded person to receive healing whenever needed. That way is through the Communion Table.

Before I leave this section, let me show you one more thing that may help you in this area.

When you look at the story of the woman with the issue of blood in the context of what was happening around Jesus, you will also see that just before the woman touched Jesus' garment, He had been asked to go with a man to heal his daughter.

Matthew 9:18–21
18 While he spake these things unto them, behold, there came a certain ruler, and worshipped him, saying, My daughter is even now dead: but come and lay thy hand upon her, and she shall live.

Notice the man's request: "Come and lay your hand on her and she will live." The man needed Jesus to **go** with him and to **touch** the daughter.

Based upon the definition of "carnal," we can see that the man was carnal-minded. He needed Jesus to go and to touch. Jesus did not need to go and to touch because we know He could just speak and it would be done.

It was the man who needed Jesus to go and touch. That was where the man's faith was set. That was his "point of contact."

19 And Jesus arose, and followed him, and so did his disciples.

An important thing to notice here is that Jesus actually went with the man, and we know that the story ends with the man's daughter being raised from the dead.

Jesus didn't belittle the man for needing Him to go and touch the daughter. Jesus was practicing what He preached. He told people He would do whatever they asked. He said they could have "whatsoever" they desired.

Several times, Jesus actually said to people who came to Him, "What do you want me to do for you?" and when they told Him, He did it.

Even a carnal-minded person can have their needs met. Then, in the next verses, we see the woman with the issue of blood approach Him and get healed. Healing was an everyday, all day practice of Jesus!

20 And, behold, a woman, which was diseased with an issue of blood twelve years, came behind him, and touched the hem of his garment:
21 For she said within herself, If I may but touch his garment, I shall be whole.

Chapter 4
Healing For The Spiritual Christian

Finally, we come to the section that will detail where most Christians want to be.

Let's start by saying that being spiritual-minded has very little to do with how much Scripture one can quote. Being spiritually minded has more to do with what you've done with the Scripture you know.

In the last section, I gave some specific examples of how the spiritually minded Christian thinks and functions in contrast to how the carnally minded Christian thinks and functions.

Before we finish this book, I will show you exactly how a Christian should think and function.

The spiritual-minded Christian is one who is having their mind renewed to think in accordance with the principles of faith and the Word of God. A renewed mind does not think, "What does the Bible say about this?"

A renewed mind simply thinks what the Bible says. A spiritual-minded Christian has already put the words of God into their mind and acted upon them to the point that it is now how they think. Let me give you an example.

If a person asks a spiritually minded Christian to pray for their sick child, the spiritually minded Christian does not go through a list of questions such as:

"God, is it Your will that I go pray for this child?"

"God, is it Your will that this child be healed?"

"What sin caused this child to be sick?"

"Was it the sin of the parents or the sin of the child that caused this sickness?"

"Is this a generational curse that needs to be broken?"

Those are all the questions of a carnally minded Christian. A spiritual-minded Christian will never ask these questions.

A spiritual-minded Christian knows God's will and focuses on it and does it. A spiritually minded Christian knows that oppression is never God's will. A spiritually minded Christian has already settled the fact of God's will and will not entertain doctrines or questions that contradict it.

A spiritually minded Christian is one who is at least in the process of renewing their mind. It may not be totally renewed yet, but there is definitely a difference in the regular, ongoing thinking of the spiritually minded Christian. (For more on this area and for specific biblical training in renewing your mind, you may want to attend my Mind Renewal Training Seminar or listen to/watch the seminar. Attendance at any of my seminars is offered free of charge.)

Now let's get into the heart of the matter.

How does the spiritual Christian receive healing?

What I am about to reveal here will absolutely change your life!

If you begin putting this into practice, there are several benefits and results that you will see come to pass, such as:

1. Any time sickness or disease tries to attach itself to you, you will be able to repel it and walk in divine health.

2. If sickness or disease actually gets a foothold in your body and you need healing, you will be able to receive healing instantly, at any time, without having to get someone else to pray for you or lay hands upon you.

3. You will become very adept at releasing the life of God and the power of God into those who need healing.

4. You will understand how to release the various manifestations of God's Spirit (normally called "gifts of the Spirit") as needed.

I taught the mechanics of this in a teaching called "Releasing the Spirit into Your Flesh." Once you learn how to release God's Spirit for healing, you will also understand how to release any gift/manifestation that is needed.

Before we look at the specific Scriptures that relate to this, let me give you some background info. Romans 8 is about several things, and there is a lot of good stuff in it.

We are going to look at several specific parts. There has also been a lot of wrong teaching that has come out of people cherry picking certain points and ignoring others.

This passage is the basis of the carnal versus spiritual discussion.

Romans 8:1–11
1 There is therefore now no condemnation to them which are in Christ Jesus, who walk not after the flesh, but after the Spirit.

Many times, people quote the first part of this verse but ignore the last part, which is the part that makes the first part true! There is no condemnation to people who do not walk after the flesh but rather walk after the spirit.

2 For the law of the Spirit of life in Christ Jesus hath made me free from the law of sin and death.

This simply says that we are under a new law: the law of the spirit of life in Christ Jesus.

3 For what the law could not do, in that it was weak through the flesh, God sending his own Son in the likeness of sinful flesh, and for sin, condemned sin in the flesh:

This says that Jesus did what the law could not.

4 That the righteousness of the law might be fulfilled in us, who walk not after the flesh, but after the Spirit.

Here is a part many miss: the righteousness of the law can and should be fulfilled in us (if and when) we walk after the spirit and not the flesh.

5 For they that are after the flesh do mind the things of the flesh; but they that are after the Spirit the things of the Spirit.

This verse describes what it means to be carnally minded or spiritually minded. It means that to think about things from a normal, natural way of thinking is to be carnal-minded. To be spiritual-minded means to think about things with the mind of the Spirit. It means to think about things the way God would think about them. It means to think in alignment with the Bible and its principles.

6 For to be carnally minded is death; but to be spiritually minded is life and peace.

This verse is very telling because it shows the difference in the results of thinking carnally or spiritually. This is a verse that has largely been ignored, but it is very important. It states the basic truths that show the value of being spiritually minded.

To dwell upon or be ruled by the normal, natural way of thinking is to be carnally minded. To dwell upon or be ruled by the word of God and thinking in alignment with it is to be spiritually minded.

7 Because the carnal mind is enmity against God: for it is not subject to the law of God, neither indeed can be.

The carnal, flesh-minded, natural-minded way of thinking is not in alignment with the ways of God and will not submit to the ways of God.

8 So then they that are in the flesh cannot please God.

Because the carnal mind will not submit to God's ways, anyone who is carnal-minded cannot please God!

9 But ye are not in the flesh, but in the Spirit, if so be that the Spirit of God dwell in you. Now if any man have not the Spirit of Christ, he is none of his.

This verse states that if the Spirit of God dwells in you and controls your mind, thoughts, and actions, then you are not walking after the fleshly, carnal mind, but rather you are walking in the Spirit.

The last part is especially important.

If you don't have the Spirit of Christ, you cannot walk in the Spirit. If you cannot walk in the Spirit, you do not belong to Christ and are lost!

10 And if Christ be in you, the body is dead because of sin, but the Spirit is life because of righteousness.

This is simply stating that if you have the Spirit of Christ, live in the Spirit, and walk in the Spirit, you will consider your body dead (meaning that it has no power or authority over you), but instead you will awaken unto righteousness and do righteousness. This is a sign that you have become spiritually minded.

11 But if the Spirit of him that raised up Jesus from the dead dwell in you, he that raised up Christ from the dead shall also quicken your mortal bodies by his Spirit that dwelleth in you.

Here's the main Scripture I want to share with you. If you remember when you got born again, you will realize that while the devil owned you, you were able to break away from him and get saved simply by believing one verse: John 3:16.

When you decided to accept Jesus as your Lord according to Colossians 1:13, you were translated (a transfer of ownership) from the power (Greek word: *exousia* = authority) of darkness and into the kingdom of God's Son.

In verse 11 above it states that IF the Spirit of the One that raised Jesus from the dead DWELLS in you, then He (the One that raised Jesus from the dead) will ALSO quicken (Strong's Concordance: New Testament: #2227 - zoopoieo (dzo-op-oy-eh'-o); from the same as NT: 2226 and NT: 4160; to (re-) vitalize (literally or figuratively): translated in the KJV - make alive, give life, quicken.

This verse is literally saying that the Spirit of God dwelling in you will give life to your mortal body. Jesus said that the Spirit in you will be rivers of living water flowing up and out of your belly (innermost being: your spirit).

Most Bible scholars, in discussing this verse, have concentrated on the fact that at some point in time, corruptible will put on incorruption (1 Corinthians 15:53-54).

Because of their focus on the future, they have not focused on the present time benefit of having the same Spirit that is going to do that living in them NOW. That Spirit is going to so completely overwhelm the physical that the very life (*zoe*) of God is going to saturate and change every cell in your physical body.

Notice that the word Jesus used to describe the life that He came to bring us is #2222 zoe (dzo-ay'); in the Strong's concordance. Life (literally or figuratively): KJV - life (-time). Every time Jesus mentioned eternal life or the kind of life (essence) that God has, He always used the word "zoe," (#2222) which is the root word for the word translated as "quicken" in Romans 8:11.

This is essentially telling us that the way God is going to cause our bodies to become incorruptible (meaning "not able to decay") is that He is going to cause His Spirit in us to so overwhelm and overtake us (from the inside out) that we will become incorruptible and at the same time we will become "immortal."

As I said, most Bible scholars agree that this will occur at a particular point in time. That point in time is generally thought to be at the time Jesus returns. I have no reason to dispute this, and it appears to be sound biblical doctrine.

I am stating all this because I want you to realize that when I am talking about releasing the Spirit of God into your flesh to bring healing, I am not referring to you becoming incorruptible or immortal. I am referring to the fact that we now have the Spirit dwelling within us as the "earnest" (down payment) of the Spirit (2 Corinthians 1:22; 2 Corinthians 5:5).

If the Spirit of God is going to completely overtake our physical body at a future point in time, to the degree that it is going to change us from mortal to immortal and corruptible into incorruptible, then surely the indwelling presence of that same Spirit can be released into our flesh and if it is, surely it would have the effect of healing our mortal flesh. Maybe this would be a good time to explain what actually happens when a person gets healed.

In the DHT (Divine Healing Technician) Training that I have done all over the world (with the same results everywhere), I explain in detail how healing is actually accomplished.

I do not have the time or space to be as detailed here, so I would strongly urge you to watch or listen to a DHT. (You can do so free of charge at: www.jglm.org)

I am going to make some blunt statements. They are biblical, and therefore true. They also go directly against the current commonly taught doctrines concerning healing.

Notice that when the woman with the issue of blood touched Jesus' garment, the Scripture says that **virtue** went out of Him. Notice that it went OUT OF HIM. It did not fall from heaven.

Mark 5:28-30

28 For she said, If I may touch but his clothes, I shall be whole.
29 And straightway the fountain of her blood was dried up; and <u>she felt in her body</u> that she was healed of that plague.
*30 And Jesus, immediately <u>**knowing in himself that virtue had gone out of him**</u>, turned him about in the press, and said, Who touched my clothes?*

Luke 8:43–48

43 And a woman having an issue of blood twelve years, which had spent all her living upon physicians, neither could be healed of any,
44 Came behind him, and **touched** *the border of his garment: and immediately her issue of blood stanched.*
45 And Jesus said, Who touched me? When all denied, Peter and they that were with him said, Master, the multitude throng thee and press thee, and sayest thou, Who touched me?
*46 And Jesus said, <u>Somebody hath touched me</u>: for I <u>perceive</u> that **<u>virtue is gone out of me.</u>**
47 And when the woman saw that she was not hid, she came trembling, and falling down before him, she declared unto him before all the people for what cause <u>she had touched him</u> and how she was healed immediately.
48 And he said unto her, Daughter, be of good comfort: thy faith hath made thee whole; go in peace.

Now look at what the Scripture says in Luke 6:17–19.

17 And he came down with them, and stood in the plain, and the company of his disciples, and a great multitude of people out of all Judaea and Jerusalem, and from the sea coast of Tyre and Sidon, which came to hear him, and <u>to be healed of their diseases;</u>

18 And they that were vexed with unclean spirits: <u>and they were healed</u>.
*19 And <u>the whole multitude sought to **touch** him</u>: for there <u>went virtue **out of him**</u>, and <u>healed them all</u>.*

What is virtue?
Every time the word "virtue" is used in reference to power or healing in Jesus' ministry, it is always the same word: *dunamis*. NT: 1411-'dunamis (doo'-nam-is); from NT: 1410; force (literally or figuratively); especially, miraculous power (usually by implication, a miracle itself).

Not once does it ever say that virtue (power) fell from heaven. Jesus was anointed with the Holy Ghost and power!

The word for *virtue* (dunamis) (power) is the same word that is used when you receive the Holy Ghost (Acts 1:8).

Acts 1:8
8 But ye shall receive power ((Greek #1411): dunamis), after that the Holy Ghost is come upon you:

The exact same power, virtue, ability, miracle-working power abides in you, dwells in you, that was in Jesus Himself.

There are several kinds of power. There is electrical power, nuclear power, combustion power (such as an automobile motor produces), and steam power, etc. "Power" simply means "ability."

God's power is: LIFE. God IS Life, and that Life produces power. When I minister to the sick, I am not technically releasing power. I am actually releasing life. I am releasing God's Life, to be specific.

Because I have the Spirit of God, which is the Spirit of Life, I am releasing Life. If I was just releasing power, then that power that destroys the sickness or disease in a person would also destroy everything else in them, thus killing them. But I don't just release power, I release life, and because I am releasing life, the life doesn't hurt the person, it only destroys the "death" that is in them.

That death is the sickness or disease. (Sickness and disease are just death in its embryonic state. If it is left alone and allowed to continue to grow, it will produce death. God's life destroys death. It drives it out.)

This is why John Lake had such great success in his healing rooms. He made the sick agree to come back every day for 30 days. Every day they would hear the word of God (the Words of Life), and every day they would have a divine healing technician lay hands on them and release life into them.

When I minister to the sick, I do not ask God to drop healing from heaven. I speak the Words of Life in a command, directing it where I desire it to go, and out of my belly flows rivers of living water.

John 7:38
He that believeth on me, as the Scripture hath said, out of his belly shall flow rivers of living water.

This Scripture literally says in the Greek:
"Out of his belly shall flow rivers of water life" (Strong's Concordance NT # 2198) Zao – life.

The life of God produces a power of its own. A different type of power, a power that kills everything that is destructive to life.

This is why when we lay hands on the sick, we can do it over and over and not be in doubt or unbelief. Every time I lay hands on the sick I am simply releasing more life into them.
If the life in me and you can flow out of us (notice it comes out of our belly, our innermost being, our spirit), then it can be released into our flesh, just as it is released into the sick person's flesh.

This is how a spiritually minded Christian gets healed. They do not need others to lay hands on them. Technically, that method was meant for the unbeliever, and was to be used as a sign that God was setting them free.

They do not need hands laid on them because when hands are laid on the sick, it is just to release the Spirit into the flesh of the sick so they can get well.

The spiritual-minded Christian knows that this is how healing flows and simply decides to release the Spirit of God dwelling in their spirit into their flesh.

The spiritual-minded Christian participates in Communion as a remembrance of what Jesus accomplished, and knows the value and the benefits of the cup and the bread. But they don't need to receive healing that way. They don't have to wait to participate in Communion to get healed. They know they can receive healing at any moment in time. They simply have to choose to release it into their body.

As the spiritual-minded Christian matures spiritually, they also realize and learn that they can live every day with the spirit flowing into their flesh, which results in divine health. The Spirit of God radiating from their spirit can repel every sickness and every disease that would try to impose itself on them.

The spiritual-minded Christian matures spiritually to a point that the Life of God radiating from them can actually heal those around them without the sick ever having to be actually touched. This is the inference in Acts 5:15–16.

Acts 5:15–16
15 Insomuch that they brought forth the sick into the streets, and laid them on beds and couches, that at the least the shadow of Peter passing by might overshadow some of them.
16 There came also a multitude out of the cities round about unto Jerusalem, bringing sick folks, and them which were vexed with unclean spirits: and they were healed every one.

It never says that Peter or anyone else laid hands on the sick. It says that they were laid out so that Peter's shadow might overshadow them. Then it says they were ALL healed. It wasn't Peter's shadow that healed them, it was the fact that the LIFE of God emanated from Peter as far as his shadow reached.

This is the basis of transfiguration that Jesus experienced (only on a smaller scale). This is why it says that Moses' face glowed so much that they had to put a veil over his face. Throughout history, artists have depicted holy men of God as emanating light.

Now modern science has also proven, through Kirlian photography, that the life of every living thing puts off a light. Perhaps this is just one part of what the Scriptures mean in John 1:4–12.

John 1:4–12

4 In him was life; and the life was the light of men.
5 And the light shineth in darkness; and the darkness comprehended it not.
6 There was a man sent from God, whose name was John.
7 The same came for a witness, to bear witness of the Light, that all men through him might believe.
8 He was not that Light, but was sent to bear witness of that Light.
9 That was the true Light, which lighteth every man that cometh into the world.
10 He was in the world, and the world was made by him, and the world knew him not.
11 He came unto his own, and his own received him not.
12 But as many as received him, to them gave he power to become the sons of God, even to them that believe on his name:

The spiritually minded Christian has a "communion" with God that brings reality to the statements of Jesus that He and The Father are one, and that we are to be one with one another and with them. This is the essence of Christianity. This is the heart and reason for the New Covenant. This is what so many Christians have yearned for, yet have been led off into other directions.

God has such a love for each and every one of us that He has made a way for any person and every person in the world to be healed.

He desires each and every person to be healed and to live healed. He wants us to prosper and be in health, even as our soul prospers.

3 John 2
Beloved, I wish above all things that thou mayest prosper and be in health, even as thy soul prospereth.

As your soul prospers, you become more spiritually minded.

Chapter 5
Whose Faith?

Have you ever been told that the reason you failed to receive God's blessing (in any area) was because you did not have enough faith?

Maybe you heard that from a relative, fellow church member, or worse yet, from a minister. Have you ever wondered why, when you failed to receive, it was your lack of faith, but when you received it was always someone else's faith or gifting or anointing that brought the results?

One of the most damaging false doctrines permeating the Body of Christ is that you cannot have faith for another person.

Now, in the area of salvation from sin this is true, because eternal life is based upon a relationship with God. But in the area of healing, this is not true, because the healing of anyone (saved or unsaved) is provided as a sign accompanying a believer (Mark 16:18).

Obviously, it would be preferable for everyone to have their own faith, but if they don't, it becomes the privilege and responsibility of the believer to have faith for them.

In Matthew 17:14–20, Jesus not only explained that the reason for their failure to heal a young boy was due to their unbelief, but he also scolded the disciples for not having faith to set the boy free. Jesus could not have expressed disapproval if He had not expected them to be able to use their faith for the boy.

When Jesus fed the multitudes it was because He took responsibility for people, just as He taught His disciples to do in Matthew 7:12.

Matthew 7:12
Therefore all things whatsoever ye would that men should do to you, do ye even so to them: for this is the law and the prophets.

If Jesus taught His disciples to live by that principle, then He too had to live by it or risk being a hypocrite. Throughout the Bible there are numerous examples of people being healed by the faith of someone else.

Abraham obviously had faith for Abimelech to be healed because we see in the following verse that God healed Abimelech in response to Abraham's prayer of faith.

Genesis 20:17

So Abraham prayed unto God: and God healed Abimelech, and his wife, and his maidservants; and they bare children.

We also see in the case of the Centurion's servant (Matthew 8) that it was the Centurion's faith that captured Jesus' attention and brought the servant's healing.

Matt 8:8, 10, 13

8 The centurion answered and said, Lord, I am not worthy that thou shouldest come under my roof: but speak the word only, and my servant shall be healed.
10 When Jesus heard it, he marvelled, and said to them that followed, Verily I say unto you, I have not found so great faith, no, not in Israel.
13 And Jesus said unto the centurion, Go thy way; and as thou hast believed, so be it done unto thee. And his servant was healed in the selfsame hour.

It is clear in this passage that it was what the Centurion believed (had faith for) that caused the power of God through Jesus' word to heal the servant.

Over and over again you will see situations in the Scriptures that point to someone having faith for someone else. For more in-depth teaching on having faith for others, please visit our website (www.jglm.org) where you may obtain a CD or MP3 download or read more articles on this and other related topics.

As I said earlier, it is always preferable that a person has their own faith for their healing or for the healing of their child or loved one. When my daughter died there was no one to have faith for me, so I decided to be that person for someone else.

Signs follow or accompany the believer to show the unbeliever God's goodness and readiness to help in any situation.

Questions and Answers About Healing
by Curry R. Blake, General Overseer
John G. Lake Ministries

Question 1:
What is the difference between JGLM and some of the other healing groups?

Some of the differences are very easy to detect, while others are more subtle. There are many different groups and teachings on healing. Some of these groups even claim some lineage back to John G. Lake.

Dr. Lake founded several organizations while he was alive (eight, to be exact); only a couple are still in existence. Of those two or three organizations, only JGLM still teaches Dr. Lake's teachings. As a matter of fact, only JGLM was given a manual used by Dr. Lake to train his Divine Healing Technicians.

Anyone who has studied under the various groups will testify to the unique authority and authenticity of what JGLM teaches as compared to the other groups.

While Dr. Lake operated Healing Rooms, his main purpose was to train Christians to minister healing anywhere. His goal was not just to open Healing Rooms, but also to train Christians to be able to demonstrate the power of God. Our focus at JGLM is exactly that: to train Christians to minister to anyone, anywhere, at any time.

Opening a Healing Room doesn't get people healed. Teaching them to walk like Jesus does.

Question 2:
What is the major difference in the area of dominion and authority?

Most groups teach a very limited authority. JGLM teaches (and proves from the Bible) that Christians are to walk in the fullness of Jesus' authority. Most of the differences are detailed in the teaching series by Reverend Blake called: "Killing Sacred Cows." Some of these topics will be included in the answers to various questions. No longer do many Christians pray for God to heal someone. They are learning to take their position in Christ and command sickness and disease and the devil to leave the sick person.

Question 3:
Does a sick person have to have their own faith to be healed?

It is generally believed and taught that each person needing healing must have their own faith for their own healing, but let's look at what the Bible reveals. There is no mention of the Roman Centurion's servant having any faith for healing. As a matter of fact, all attention is put on authority. The Roman Centurion said he knew Jesus could heal because he understood authority. Jesus said that the man had the greatest faith he had ever found; so one aspect of the greatest faith is to understand authority. <u>It is very clear that the Roman Centurion had faith for his servant.</u>

The Syrophonecian woman came to Jesus on behalf of her daughter. There is no indication in Scripture that the daughter had any faith for her deliverance. Jesus said that the woman had great faith and that because of her great faith, her daughter was healed. <u>The woman had faith for her daughter.</u>

Four men were carrying their paralytic friend on a stretcher to Jesus; the Scriptures state that Jesus saw "their" faith. The grammatical structure of the Scripture proves that the "their" Jesus referred to was the four men, not the man being carried. <u>The four men had faith for the paralytic.</u>

When Jesus raised Lazarus from the dead, whose faith was it that did the raising? Who had faith for Lazarus? It wasn't Lazarus. <u>Jesus had faith for Lazarus.</u>

When Peter healed the lame man at the Beautiful Gate, there was no mention of the man having faith for healing. Peter said, "What I have I give you, IN THE NAME OF JESUS." (That is what Peter had.) "Rise up and walk." Peter gave an authoritative command. He took the man by the hand and lifted him and the man was healed. Later, Peter gave the secret to healing when he said, "It was the Name of Jesus that made this man whole and faith in that Name." Who had faith in that Name? It was Peter. <u>Peter had faith for the man's healing.</u>

Question 4:
Does a person have to have their own faith for their own healing?

The answer FROM THE BIBLE, obviously is NO. However, should a person have their own faith for their own healing? Sure.

That is a good thing. One reason is because if you do not have your own faith for your own healing, you will always be at the mercy of someone else. You will always be relying on someone else's faith, and you can never be sure that they are where they should be in relation to having faith in God for you.

Besides, if you do not have your own faith for your own healing, how are you going to be ready to have faith for someone else's healing? Christians must stop being spiritual hitchhikers and start to have their own faith, not only for themselves, but also for the others that need help.

Secondly, why would you need someone to lay hands on you or minister to you if it is your faith that is going to do the job?

In James 5:14–15, it clearly shows that the ONLY responsibility the sick person has is to CALL FOR THE ELDERS. That is the extent of the sick person's "faith." Once the elders get there, the responsibility becomes theirs to pray the prayer of faith.

Now, if they are going to pray the prayer of faith, who is supposed to be having the faith? If you don't have faith, how can you pray the prayer of faith?

Notice: it does not say that the person's faith will heal the sick. It says that the prayer of faith (prayed by the elders) SHALL SAVE (HEAL) THE SICK. This verse also proves that if the sick person has sin in their life, IT WILL NOT STOP THE FAITH OF THE ELDERS NOR THE POWER OF GOD. The person will be forgiven and healed. (More on this topic later.)

The teaching that each person has to have their own faith was originally thought up by the devil, then passed on to preachers who could not produce the power of God, so they had to have a spiritual reason why the sick person was not healed. And since they could not take the blame or people would lose faith in them, they turned it on the people and blamed them for not having faith. But when a minister lays hands on someone and they get healed, see how fast the minister takes credit for having the faith that healed them.

When Jesus saw faith in a person, He commended it; when He didn't, He merely had faith for them and fixed their problem. The only people Jesus ever "blasted" for not having faith were His own disciples, and religious hypocrites.

When Jesus blasted His disciples, it wasn't because they did not have faith to get healed, it was because they did not have faith to heal others.

Some would say, "But what about the Scripture that says Paul saw that the man had faith to be healed, so Paul healed him?" The Scripture where Paul recognized faith in the man and the Scripture where Peter just healed a man without any faith on the man's part proves my point.

If a person has faith, wonderful; if a person doesn't, you have faith for them.

Question 5:
I have heard ministers tell the parents of children born with handicaps that the reason their child wasn't healed was because they (the parents) didn't have enough faith. Is that true?

First, I would like to say that if I ever heard a minister—or anyone else, for that matter—say something like that to a parent of a handicapped or sick child, I would immediately and publicly rebuke that minister, and I would not hesitate for one second. Anyone who can be that unfeeling, uncaring, and hard-hearted has no business being in the ministry. They are a Pharisee, putting burdens on people even they couldn't bear. I would hope that any "minister" saying such a thing would just be ignorant and repeating what he had been taught. But at the very least, that kind of statement would eliminate that person from having any spiritual input into my life. If I heard it preached from a pulpit, I would walk out of the service right then, with my entire family leaving with me.

If a minister tells anyone that their child failed to be healed because of a lack of faith, I hope the parents or some bold saint will speak up and demand that the minister have faith to produce the child's healing right then. That would make most of them at least think twice before spouting such garbage.

Now let's get back to the heart of the question. What about the child? Every parent should have faith for their own children, and even their own family members. God gave the child to that parent, so that parent has a responsibility to have faith in God for their children.

But if they don't, it is not the proper thing to point the finger or fix blame. As Christians and as ministers, we are to bear the burdens of those who are "weaker." So don't ever tell people they don't have enough faith; have faith for them. Then teach them how to have faith.

Question 6:
I have heard some ministers even say that if a child was born with a handicap that it somehow was the parents' fault. Is this true?

There are several possible reasons for children to be born with a handicap, sickness, or deformity.

One reason is that certain genetic traits may be present, because we live in a sin-infested world with germs, bacteria, viruses, and etc. "Things happen."

Now, let me expound a little on that. This may be true of a non-Christian, but it <u>should</u> never be the case with a Christian parent.

Notice: "should." The devil is like a very crooked lawyer that will find out if you know what your inheritance includes, and if you do not know, he will rob you of that inheritance, and you will think it is normal, or at the worst, believe it came from God. There are times when the parents are zealous Christians and may or may not know that they do not have to have a child with any physical problems. They may be doing a good work for God, so the devil tries to stop them or slow them down by attacking them through their child's health. This may happen at birth or after.

Sometimes, a genetic or physical problem can be brought on by certain substances that were indulged in by one or both of the parents before the child was born or during the pregnancy. This can include drugs, tobacco, and/or alcohol. It can also be by breathing "toxic" fumes, so in that sense, yes, a child's situation can be brought on by the parents. BUT, we in the ministry ARE NOT DOCTORS. Our job is not to diagnose or to fix blame, but rather to fix the problem. Set the oppressed free. Jesus never pointed out the sick person's problem. He simply set them free.

This is also an area where the topic of generational curses comes up. We will deal with generational curses later in a section all its own. But let me say this: If you are in

Christ, Christ has become a curse for you and redeemed you from the curse. If there is no condemnation in Christ Jesus to those who walk not after the flesh, but after the Spirit, then surely there is no (generational) curse in Christ Jesus. The Scriptures say that once you are dead, you are free from the law and therefore, free from the curse of the law. If you are in Christ, you are dead. You no longer live, but Christ lives in you.

Secondly, how can you have a generational curse when your only "generation" is from God? You are now your Heavenly Father's son or daughter, so from whence does a generational curse come? If you say you have a generational curse, you are actually saying you are not born again and you are of your father, the devil.

Some would say that what they mean by a generational curse is that if their earthly father was an alcoholic, then the curse of that sin will come down to them. Each person is responsible for THEIR OWN SIN, NOT THEIR PARENTS' SIN. When Jesus' disciples asked Him who did sin, was it the one born blind or was it the person's father, Jesus answered, "Neither." That would have been a perfect time for Jesus to teach on generational curses. That was the closest He ever got to teaching on this subject. What most people call generational curses are nothing more than sins they are committing. If people were taught correctly about the new birth and what it entails, we would not be dealing with this subject at all; but then how would all those book writers get people's money? The topic of generational curses has become an industry of its own, with books, seminars, counselors, etc.

I recently heard one well-known TV preacher from Portland, Oregon (who also has a church in Dallas, Texas), tell the people that now it's not enough to simply rebuke a curse. "YOU MUST SEND THOSE CURSES BACK TO WHOEVER SENT THEM ON YOU." Unfortunately, most of the people in the audience were too caught up in the emotional moment to examine what he said in the light of clear Scripture. Jesus said, "Bless them that curse you." At some point, Christians are going to have to realize that just because a person is on TV or has a book out, it does not mean they are right. It only means that they have money, usually the money they got from gullible Christians.

Question 7:
If I take medicine after being prayed for, will it stop my healing?

I do not believe that there is any medicine that is stronger than God's power. In the early days of the Pentecostal Movement, there were serious problems stemming from the medical practices of the day (as there are today). The teaching that taking medicine will stop healing is based upon the belief that if you are prayed for, you must then act as though you are healed, and a healed person does not need medicine, so to continue taking the medicine after being prayed for actually showed that the person did not really believe that they were healed.

Dr. Lake once testified in court, under oath, that his people did not need anyone to tell them not to go to doctors; they had enough sense to figure that out on their own. Dr. Lake had studied medicine and concluded that all medical practice was guesswork. His biggest enemies in the Pacific Northwest were the doctors and the Health Department officials.

He once told his congregation that if they had any medicine they should dump it into the toilet and then apologize to the toilet.

I applaud the stand Dr. Lake and other early Pentecostal pioneers took concerning doctors and medicine; however, I believe that we should help lift and encourage people and not say things that put them under condemnation if they are not walking at that level of consecration or understanding. Again, if the ministers will begin to have faith for people, then the people can be healed and then taught how to walk in divine health. I do not believe we should try to force a certain discipline upon people from the outside; that is called legalism. It is far better to simply preach the Word of God and let the people see the possibility and the standards of God, and let them rise to that level on their own.

Question 8:
Why do some ministers who preach healing wear glasses?

First, let's get something straight. No one has a right to base their interpretation of Scripture on the walk of another person. You should never base what you believe God wants you to do on what another person does. A wise person will always look at the Word of God for their example and for their "limitations." Men make mistakes; people who base their walk with God on how another person walks with God will always fall, eventually. Quit looking for examples and become one. Now, let's move on to the question.

A minister can preach healing and yet not have a good understanding of why or how God heals. He may believe that God will heal others and yet not be convinced that God will heal him. He may be committing some secret sin, large or small, and therefore believe that God won't heal him until he quits the sin. Notice the important thing here is that he BELIEVES that God won't heal him until he quits the sin. If that is what he believes, then that is what he will receive. Everyone gets from God "according as they have believed."

Many ministers believe that their eye problems are their "thorn in the flesh," just as they believed that Paul's thorn in the flesh was an eye problem.

We will deal with "Paul's Thorn" in a later question.

Ministers are not exempt from God's demand that we live by faith. Being a minister doesn't mean that you have fewer problems than other people; it means you bear their burdens and your own problems and situations. Ministers who preach healing, many times have to fight sickness and disease in their own bodies, more often than the people they pray for. Now this is not God's plan; it is how the enemy works. The Bible principle is that the laborer should be the first partaker of what he preaches. The fact that a healing minister would continue to preach healing while wearing eyeglasses should be a tribute to his fortitude rather than a detraction.

If a minister's glasses bother you, pray for him; don't badmouth him. But if you are going to pray for him, do it between God and you. Don't go to him and bring it up; he is likely already fighting the devil, who constantly tries to put condemnation on ministers (just like he does everybody else). The enemy will constantly barrage (buffet) a minister with the idea of getting out of the ministry by making the minister feel that he is not living up to the standard of the Word of God and the message he preaches. Don't help the devil. Pray privately for the minister. Even if you go to him and offer to pray for him, the enemy will try to turn your concern into condemnation. So pray for him in your prayer closet. This same principle would hold true with any physical problems that a minister may be dealing with.

Question 9:
Why do many ministers who preach healing have sick family members?

Many times, the hardest people to reach and to minister to are those of your own household. Some have said that each sick person must have their own faith, so if a family member is sick, it is up to them to have their own faith. We have already destroyed that myth in the answer to a previous question.

Just as in the situation of a child and its parent, there can be several factors involved with the healing of a family member.

The first thing to consider is: has the healing minister actually ministered to the family member?

The second is that a minister can get a family member healed, but it is up to the family member to stay healed. Jesus said in John 14:4, "Go and sin no more lest a worse thing come upon thee." You don't necessarily know if the minister has prayed for the family member and they got healed, but they continued in a practice that brought the illness back. Divine healing isn't immunity from every sickness or disease from then on. It is simply an event that changed the immediate situation. It is then up to the healed person to get in the Word of God and get the Word of God in them.

As stated previously, you must never judge the Word of God or a ministry on anything other than the message that is being brought forth.

The families of healing ministers often go through tremendous trials and sufferings, not because it is God's will, but because "persecution comes for the Word's sake." When you walk in the truth of God's Word, your life situations will change; many times for what appears to be the worse. Now the enemy has you on his radar. Previously, you were just a face in the crowd, going along in the same manner as everyone else. But when you start to truly walk as Jesus walked, get ready for some persecution from the enemy like he brought against Jesus.

Again, if you see the family member of a healing minister who has a physical sickness or situation, don't embarrass them by approaching them and asking things like, "Why are you are sick if what your husband teaches is real?" or, "Why do you wear glasses if what your husband teaches is true?" Every person has their own battles to fight. I promise you, the spouses of healing ministers are constantly on the battlefront. They are constantly wearing a bull's-eye target, because many times they are not as active in ministering healing as their spouse.

The enemy sees them as a sitting target and the minister as a moving target. Well, it's always easier to hit a sitting target than it is a moving target. Pray for the families of healing ministers. Many times, because of their spouse's prominence, they feel that they cannot ask for prayer because it might cause someone to lose faith. (I am not saying this is a correct way to feel, I am just saying that it happens.)

Question 10:
How many times can you raise someone from the dead?

You continue praying and commanding as many times as you are willing to stay there with them and continue working with them.

Question 11:
How long can a person be dead before it is impossible to raise them up?

"According to your faith, be it unto you."

Question 12:
Didn't healing pass away with the apostles?

There is not one Scripture that leads us to believe that healing passed away with the apostles. The powers that the apostles had were not because they were apostles, but because they were Christians building the Church. There are essentially only two time periods in Scripture: the Old Covenant time and the New Covenant time. The apostles operated under the New Covenant. We are still in the time of the New Covenant. The New Covenant is a better covenant built upon better promises. Jesus said He would never leave us, even until the end of the world (age). The "age" referred to is the age of the New Covenant.

Question 13:
How old do you have to be to heal the sick or raise the dead?

The younger you are, the more likely you are to actually do something. The younger you are, the less you have to be untaught. This holds true until you reach the age of a senior citizen. Usually by then you have reached a point where you no longer care what people think, so you will start to step out more. This problem is often caused by not having received proper teaching. Many are actually waiting for a specific word from God before they will step out. Imagine that your parents were going away for the weekend and before they left, they wrote down some specific instructions as to what you were to do while they were gone. Then when they returned, none of the things were done. When they asked why you didn't do them, you answered, "I wasn't sure you meant that I was supposed to do them. I thought if you had wanted me to do them, you would have called me and told me to do what you had written down." Do you think that would have worked, or do you think they would have called you disobedient?

Question 14:
Why do some people who have a lot of physical problems only get healed of one thing when they are prayed for?

That's either what they were believing for when they were prayed for or it is what the person who prayed for them was believing for. Many times people do not tell the minister or the person praying all their problems. Often they only mention a thing or two. I have actually had people tell me to only pray for one or two serious things because they can live with the other problems. I try to explain to them that if God will heal one or two serious things, He can also heal the more minor problems.

Question 15:
What about long-distance prayer? Can a person be healed even if they are not present with the person they are praying for?

Jesus healed the Roman Centurion's servant from a distance and He healed the Syrophonecian woman's daughter from a distance, so yes, a person can be healed even if they are not present. I generally tell people that since faith works by love, your faith will reach a person (and heal them) as far away as your love can reach them. If you can love a person around the world, you can have faith for a person around the world. Sometimes it is actually easier to have faith for a person who is not right in front of you. If they are in front of you, you may find reasons that would make you think they should not be healed. They may talk you out of faith.

Question 16:
Why did Jesus only heal one man at the Pool of Bethesda?

In John 5, we are given the story of the healing at the Pool of Bethesda. Please remember, the Apostle John himself said that if everything Jesus did had been written down, the world could not contain the books.

First, we are not told how many Jesus healed at the pool. We are simply told the details of one particular healing so that we can learn something from it.

We are also not told that Jesus ONLY healed the one man, so any speculation is just that; speculation. I have heard preachers describe how Jesus stepped over this person and around another person just to get to that one man. All of that is made up and added to the Bible. The very Scripture people use to try to prove that God/Jesus picks and chooses who they will heal proves just the opposite.

At the beginning of John 5, it points out that the Pool of Bethesda was a well-known place of healing and that at a certain season (most scholars believe that season to be the Passover season, which would line up with the Biblical doctrine of Healing in the Atonement), an angel would come down and "trouble" the water of the pool. When that happened, THE FIRST PERSON THAT GOT IN, GOT HEALED OF WHATSOEVER (disease/sickness/malady) THEY HAD.

This proves that God did not determine who got healed, when they got healed, or what they got healed from.

This proves God does not dictate the time of a person's healing (there goes the "It's not God's timing" doctrine).

This proves that God did not determine that some people should keep their illness until they had learned something (There there goes the "I'm sick because God's trying to teach me something" doctrine).

This proves that God does not will some to be healed and for others to stay sick (there goes the "It's not God's will to heal everybody" doctrine). Notice that there is no mention of repentance from sin. This story proves that the Passover (Jesus) is our total freedom from sickness and disease.

Question 17:
How can we expect to heal everyone if Jesus couldn't even heal everyone in his hometown?

This question comes up very often. Most people cannot quote five verses that promise healing, yet even non-Christians know of the Scriptures that seem to say that Jesus tried to heal people in His own hometown and couldn't, or that Paul had some mysterious illness or eye problem and God told him no when he asked God to heal him. (We will cover this in depth later.) They know that Paul left somebody sick somewhere but they don't remember who or where, and they know Paul told Timothy to drink some wine because of his stomach problems. We will cover all these things.

First, nowhere does the Bible say that Jesus "tried and failed" to heal anyone. Actually, it says just the opposite: "and he healed them ALL."

The Scripture in question here does not say, "Jesus tried to heal those of His own hometown, but He could not heal anyone," even though that is what is preached many times.

What it does say is: "He could there do no mighty works because of their unbelief, EXCEPT He laid His hands on a few sick folk and healed them."'(The ones He laid hands on WERE HEALED.) So you could say that He healed THEM ALL (all the ones He laid hands on).

The word "except" means that there were some mighty works that did occur, so what mighty works did not occur?
No one got healed by touching the hem of His garment; no one came to Him and asked Him to heal their child or their servant from a distance. (Refer back to the Roman Centurion and the Syrophonecian woman, both of whom Jesus said had "great faith.") Apparently no one in Nazareth got healed on their own faith but rather on the

faith of Jesus. The unbelief of the people of Nazareth likely kept them from coming to Jesus to be healed. (People who don't believe in you or are "offended" in you as they were at Jesus, don't usually come to your meetings to be healed by you.)

CERTIFIED DIVINE HEALING TECHNICIAN (DHT) STATUS

Over the past 20 years, over 100,000 people have been trained in the material presented in DHT seminars.

As you have seen, this material is vastly different from what has been recently presented to the Body of Christ, generally speaking.

Many have attended the DHT seminar with the purpose of being able to hang a certificate on their wall after merely attending. In the early days, we presented attendees with a certificate of completion.

In many cases, we later learned they were using the certificate and the seminar attendance to claim affiliation with us, yet we had not heard from them since the seminar, which in many cases was several years previous. In many cases they had associated themselves with other organizations, yet claimed the John G. Lake name or the Divine Healing Technician status while practicing other material.

Because of that, we have had to adapt our certification practices.

How To Be Certified As A Divine Healing Technician©

1. Complete a JGLM Divine Healing Technician Training Seminar, conducted by a certified JGLM DHT trainer, by DVD, or in person.

2. Fill out an application to become a Certified Divine Healing Technician on our website at www.jglm.org

3. Fill out and send in a DHT Monthly Report (see back of DHT Manual or online at: www.jglm.org) for three consecutive months.

4. Become a partner with JGLM.
Contact partners@jglm.org for more information.

5. Pay the Divine Healing Technician certification fee.

What <u>The Bible</u> Says About Divine Healing

1. Divine healing is the right and responsibility of every Christian.

2. Any hindrance to the healing of any Christian is not of God.

3. God is not our problem, He is our help.

4. Any hindrance to healing is on the part of the enemy.

5. Any sickness or disease can be overcome by a Christian if the Christian will exercise faith and power.

6. The enemy is not a serious hindrance and can be overcome by any Christian using the available tools and weapons provided by God.

7. The enemy can only be truly defeated by spiritual weapons and not by carnal/natural weapons devised by man.

8. Christians and non-Christians, without faith for healing, can be healed when Christians exercise kingdom authority.

9. All sickness and disease is a work of the enemy and is to be defeated whenever and wherever they are encountered.

Curry R. Blake (JGLM) Basic Principles

These principles will be followed by all JGLM ministers and adherents. Failure to follow these basic principles will be cause for disciplinary action up to and including revocation of credentials and affiliation.

These basic principles are non-negotiable!

1. JGLM does not comment concerning your use of medical treatment.

2. JGLM does not write "begging letters" asking for finances.

3. JGLM does not receive offerings of any kind during healing services.

4. JGLM does not receive payment or money of any kind for praying or ministering to the sick. (If money is offered before or after ministry [prayer] it will not be received.)

5. JGLM does not blame the sick or their relatives for failure to receive healing.
As far as JGLM is concerned, the failure rests upon the "Pray-er."

6. JGLM does not dig into people's past or try to find their "sins" before setting them free.

7. JGLM does not try to find a sick person's "generational curses." JGLM sets the captives free, not find out why they are a captive.

8. JGLM does not blame the parents for their child's illness or for failure to be healed.

9. JGLM does not "blend" teachings that contradict Biblical principles with the basic teachings of the JGLM Divine Healing Technician Training©.

10. JGLM does not lift up any human, nor blindly follow any human.

11. JGLM recognizes Jesus alone as the only "special" one.

The History of John G. Lake Healing Rooms

The John G. Lake Healing Rooms were originally started in 1914, when Dr. Lake began teaching on the subject of Divine Healing in a local church in Spokane, Washington.

Dr. Lake rented a group of rooms in the Rookery Building that he converted into "Lake's Healing Rooms." He began praying for the sick on a daily basis, and soon became so overwhelmed by the sheer numbers of those coming for healing that he was forced to train others in what he called "The Science of Divine Healing." The people he trained were of various ages and were both men and women. They were taken through a series of lectures on divine healing that were designed to impart faith and knowledge to bring healing to the sick. The group of men and women that Lake trained were called Divine Healing Technicians. These technicians were trained daily by both teaching and hands-on practical application.

According to Gordon Lindsay, Dr. Lake had an ability to impart faith into his hearers. He did this by teaching what he knew to be true from the Word of God concerning divine healing and the authority of the believer. Dr. Lake continued ministering in Spokane until 1920. From 1915 until 1920, the team of 16 Divine Healing Technicians and Dr. Lake recorded over 100,000 healings. Dr. Lake left Spokane in May of 1920 to go to Portland, Oregon, to begin a duplicate work there.

When Lake left Spokane, the Healing Rooms in the Rookery Building ceased operating. When Dr. Lake returned to Spokane in 1931, he set about to re-establish a church and the healing rooms. Dr. Lake passed away in 1935 and **the Healing Rooms never opened again. The original building that housed the Healing Rooms burned and a new building, bearing the same name and address, was built on the same site. Dr. Lake never set foot in the present building.**

In 1995, Reverend Curry Blake, General Overseer of John G. Lake Ministries, began plans to go to Spokane and re-open the Healing Rooms but was informed that the original building no longer existed. After a time of intense prayer and seeking the will of God, the Lord spoke and said not to focus on buildings and shrines but to carry the Spirit of the ministry.

In 1999, what is now called "Healing Rooms Ministries" opened in the **new building.** A recent earthquake, the first to hit Spokane in over 75 years, caused only one building in Spokane to be condemned, the new Rookery Building. Reverend Blake prophesied this

during a meeting in Harrisburg, Pennsylvania, less than two weeks before it happened.

"Healing Rooms Ministries" at Spokane are NOT affiliated with John G. Lake Ministries, nor are the teachings the same.

In 1997, Curry R. Blake trained and certified the first Divine Healing Technicians (DHTs) in 62 years. Those DHTs, along with the thousands who have been trained since, are experiencing the same success in divine healing that the first DHTs did under John G. Lake.

Prophetic Word Given By John G. Lake Thursday, May 24, 1934–Spokane, Washington

(Given during testimony service at Apostolic Tabernacle, Lincoln and Main.)

There shall come upon the church great darkness. The ground gained from the enemy shall be lost and false teachers shall arise and false prophets whose words shall have a ring of truth but will have no substance. They are those who will follow after gain, and greed shall be their God. They shall show forth works but their visions will not exalt Me, saith God, but their own selves and doctrines. Against this there shall come forth by My Spirit a young man, another voice crying in the wilderness to make straight the way of The Lord, restoring old ways and shoring up the terrible gap in the wall to stop the incoming flood of sin and worldliness that shall surely be in the Church in that day. This one will be rejected of men and his brethren will not understand nor accept him.

I will fill him with My Spirit, with My mind. His words shall be My words, his thoughts, my thoughts. I shall pour forth through him revelations that will be the keys to the ark of divine knowledge.

His life will be precious to Me, for his spirit will bring forth from My Spirit and show his generation of My fullness. He shall be born when this country has stopped growing, for I will bring him forth in the very last days. He shall consecrate himself to Me even as he was consecrated as a child. He will not hearken to the voices that would hinder him, for he is separated unto the work whereunto I have called him.

He will dwell upon Me night and day. I will remove any hindrances that will place itself against My purposes. I will use him mightily, for he shall not only continue the flow of this ministry, but he shall carry it to even greater depths. His heart and mind will be for the church, and he will build it up as father teaches and trains a son.

The great works that have been seen will appear as naught, for I will do greater works through him, for he is meek and seeks peace. I will cause the pride of life to pass from him and the spirit of achievement instilled in him at an early age, I will cause to leave.

The enemy will try to kill him a score and five years from my death. Before his second score of years, he shall see all these things begin. Thus saith The Lord.

John G. Lake's Letter To Carrie Judd Montgomery

April 22, 1911

Mrs. Carrie Judd Montgomery,
Beulah Heights, Alameda Co.,
Oakland, CA., U.S.A.

Dear Sister in Christ:

Enclosed find some letters with incidents etc., of what the Lord is doing among us. Rev. Stephenson has arranged for us with a friend, for the circulation of the letter which you find enclosed.

I regard it as a striking example of the force with which this Gospel comes to people of open mind, and was pleased to have a man of his caliber concerning the work. Of course he viewed the work on a day when the Spirit of God was moving mightily. It was an extraordinary day, therefore it is only fair to say that all our meetings do not have the same degree of power that was in that one.

However, we praise God that He is moving strong and steady and clearly. I am reminded to write you through the reading of Mrs. Anderson's testimony as it appears in the "Triumphs of Faith."

I haven't a copy of a letter I wrote some time ago to a missionary by the name of Hoover, at Valparaiso, Chile, on the subject of divine healing, which embodies what I regard as the secret of the aggressive ministry of healing that the Pentecostal Movement of South Africa demonstrates.

I do not know that I will be able to send you a copy of that letter at this time, but at my earliest convenience will have a copy prepared and send it to you.

I feel, Sister, that there is a step in this ministry in advance of what the (Pentecostal) Movement in general enjoys, and God has laid it deeply on my soul to present this particular phase of the exercise of the dominion of Jesus Christ, and that the secret of our success here in this ministry is in our teaching our workers to exercise the dominion of God through the Holy Ghost, and that He has already put in their soul when He baptized them; while in other branches of this work they still follow largely the old line of intercession for the sick.

We do not pray for God to come and heal as in the old days. But, looking into His face, believing that He has baptized us in the Holy Ghost, and that we have received the power of God through that baptism, command in the Name of Jesus, the devil and his works to depart.

Nevertheless, dear sister, there are instances when God puts the Spirit of real intercession, even for the sick, upon you.

I am convinced that there is a secret and better place of interceding for the sick, in exercising a dominion of God over the devil and his sicknesses, that when learned by the Pentecostal Movement, will put the ministry of healing miles in advance of where it is now.

"His name, through faith in His name, hath made this man strong." "Such as I have, give I thee." "Aeneas, Jesus maketh thee whole." We have never caught the force of Jesus' words. "Proclaim liberty to the captive." "Whatsoever thou shalt loose on earth, shall be loosed in heaven."

It was through the healing of a young man from Detroit, Michigan, in your Faith Home at Buffalo, that my interest for this ministry was first captured.

It was not until many years afterward when, through the teaching of John Alexander Dowie, I really grasped the thing so that the knowledge of the ministry became vital.

And it was only after I had received the baptism in the Holy Ghost that the dominion of God entered my soul, that compelled me to command sickness and the devil to leave, rather than to intercede with the Lord to take them away.

JGL/elw
(John G. Lake / Emma Louise Wick)
Your brother in Christ,
John G. Lake

How to Enter the Will of God
by: John G. Lake

How to Enter the Will of God – Two Phases

There are two phases to entering into the Will of God. The first is the surrender of our will to do the Will of God.

Most people's conception of doing the Will of God is to become a non-entity. Now, it is not God's ideal for you to have to be pushed around like a machine, or moved like a mechanism.

The other is recognizing yourself as God's son and man's servant. I think the most wonderful exhibition of this truth that God can give us is in the fact that He gives us the Holy Ghost to use for God.

For instance, the Lord says, "They shall lay hands on the sick, and they shall recover." But if you do not lay your hands upon anyone, they will not be healed.

However, if you have faith to believe you have the Holy Spirit to be used by Him and for Him, your heart and your hands will be ready.

It is a sad thing to me that God has to go out on a special mission and hunt a soul up and wrestle with him in order to get him to do something for God.

There used to be a Bible school in Ohio where they waited in continuous prayer meeting for nine months for the gifts of the Holy Ghost.

I said to them, "It seems to me if you stay around for ten years and nine months you will miss the Gifts of the Holy Ghost. But if you take off your coat and go out and use what God has given you to bless others, He will give you more."

Prophecy to Curry Blake
by Bishop Bill Hamon

Son, you have some things set before Me that have been a cry in your heart for a number of years that you have not voiced or shared with other people, but you are going to begin to see that the answers that I have for you are going to become a real living revelation to you. You have had a measure of revelation even in healing, but I am taking you to deeper places of revelation that are even going to begin to blow your mind.

But as it comes forth you are going to say, God, this is what I have been crying out for. This is what I have been looking for. And even as the books are written, each will be a piece to the puzzle that you have been trying to solve. You have been putting pieces together here and pieces together there. You will begin to see the pieces all coming together in greater unity. And even as you step out into deeper places of healing and step into places where you will see even more people raised from the dead just by you walking past them.

Son, there are also some relational things that you have set before me that I am going to begin to resurrect from those dead places and bring into a place of life and purpose and destiny in me, and even those people who you thought would never come into the kingdom will come in and they will even work alongside of you. Those who many years ago did not understand what you were doing, they turned and walked away. This is the day of reconciliation, this is the day of restitution, this is the day where you will begin to see them coming back to you, repenting for their attitude and repenting for the fact that they misunderstood. They will ask you to mentor them and train them and equip them.

Son, you will raise up many people who will be the reproducers of reproducers, and you will see that the work will be a quick work and it will be an even quicker work that you have had to labor to do because you have plowed the ground and made the way and now is the time for that **next generation** to step in. Even as your grandchildren begin to step into places of healing you will see healing and deliverance and great victory, even in nations will come forth from the words of your grandchildren because the anointing upon them will be more than double of what is upon you.

It will be greater than even you would envision. But son, it will be greater than all that you have ever wanted.

For surely says the Lord, son, this is a season, a time that you are coming into that you are going to reap the harvest of seeds that you have sown in your late teens and early twenties. The roots of the seeds that you have sown have grown and become this huge thing and it is a blessing that is not only going to impact you in your soul, mind, body, and spirit. I see it being something that will restore the energy and restore the things and the areas where you may have grown tired. Part of the benefit and the reaping of the harvest that you are getting is a physical reaping of your body's rejuvenation, but also where you have seen miracles with people in the physical realm and seen miracles happen before your eyes.

The Lord says, son, I am going to supernaturally bring money and finances into your life. I see someone coming into your life who is of great financial stature and will be connected with your ministry and your call and your purpose and your plan. He will know the root of what you are trying to do in the ministry and the obedience that you walk in with the Father. The Lords says, son, this person is going to be someone who supports you in whatever you need. I see checks after checks being written and the finances being there.

The Lord says, son, I am opening new doors for your family, even as your family starts to travel more and more with you. The Lord says, son, I am bringing a new, deeper, fresh relationship between your family and what is going to happen, and I see a zeal within your children rising up a passion to receive that double portion anointing and the plowing and to see their eyes being open to the sacrifices you have made throughout your life where you have set things aside, where you have wanted different things at different times and you said Lord, I receive your will and I am going to be obedient to you no matter what it is I set aside right now.

I see your family's appreciation growing for seeing your sacrifices and what it is you have given up and sacrificed. The Lord says, even though you have done that since you were a teen, this is the time when you are going to reap the harvest, not only financially, but physically and relationally with your family. I see where there has been estrangement between family members, where they have had questions and the answers have not been right according to what they wanted to hear.

But the Lord says, son, you are going to be back in that situation again and son, just lay it all on the line with them. And I see the situation turning around and even them doing the partnering in with you that you thought would never have been possible because of the way they presented themselves. Son, sit back, just receive from me. This is a time of joy. This is a time of reaping the harvest for the seed sown and the sacrifices made.

The Lord says, son, receive it. Sit back and relax, for I am going to bless you; I am going to bring what you need. This is a time to ask for even great, great, bigger things than you can imagine. I don't know if it is airplanes or whatever it is that comes into the ministry but the Lord says now is the time to ask for that. But it is in the Spirit that now is the time for the release for that. The Lord says, son I am there for you and I am going to bring it, and now is the time for the reaping of the harvest.

My son, I sense the urgency within your spirit because I have placed that urgency there. Even though, son, there are things that you have done that no one else has done, there are still things you know you can do. There are even teachings that you have done that you have not even released yet because in your study of the people who walked with Me twenty, thirty, or forty years, a hundred years ago, you saw some things there that are not ready to be revealed yet. Son, now is the time to reveal those teachings. Now is the time to reveal those revelations. And even though the disappointments in your relationship have come about here in the last two years, it is going to be taken care of. It is not going to have to be a burden on you. Son, release that burden on you. That is not your burden, My son; that is My burden. I took that burden from your shoulders. I am taking it off your shoulders.

Son, you are a man of integrity. You have people who have been looking at you for the past five years who are not sure where you are standing, but now they are sure where you are standing and now your finances will be coming in and the plane that was spoken of will be brought to you because, son, your time travel has to be decreased and your time teaching has to be increased, and that is the way it is going to be done, son.

You will be going not just from country to country but you will be going from nation to nation. You will get phone calls from presidents and princes wanting you to come to their nations. They will be Muslim nations. They will be radical nations. They will be nations that don't even know who Jesus is. But they are going to be hearing from you and people they trust, and they have some things and issues and physical healings that need to be healed. You will be able to turn around nations and make decisions in the spirit that will change the political direction of different nations.

Although you are going to be looking for things to do further, I will have people walking side by side with you. It was spoken before that your children and grandchildren will be doing marvelous works. It will set within you the desire to keep doing more, but there are times when I will hold the reins on you and will pull you back, fast, too, quickly, and if you go too quickly you will be bypassing people. There are things that have to come across your path so slowly.

This year is your year. This is the year that you will thrive and not strive. You have been striving and striving, but now you are going to thrive and not strive, because you need to have fluidity around you. Even though your martial arts shows your fluidity there is a fluidity of the Spirit that you have not yet attained. This is the year that will show that fluidity, and once that fluidity is attained, the calling on your life will be increased and your strength, your vitality, and purpose will be revealed.

I have a purpose for you that is going to be revealed. You have had a taste of it. I have not told you about it but you have sensed in the Spirit that I am going to speak to you. When I speak those words and I give you that unction, there is going to be a quick move and you will be staying within a country for three months, and during that stay there will be a change within that country that you will know what your new calling is and you will know what needs to be done.

I've searched the whole earth through. I've gone to places with you. I've found your heart. I've seen your heart. I know your heart is true. For My eyes are upon you, My son. I've come to support you, My son.

I'm clothing you this day, says the Lord, for My angels have come to you. I'm strengthening you. I'm restoring you. I'm causing you to be strong. Look up, says the Lord your God, for today I am opening My heavens. You will have what you need. You will ask what you need. You will have what you need, says the Lord. Look up and see My face. Look up and see My face, for you have my attention. You have my voice. You have My will. You will have My way. Look up, says the Lord your God. For I have shaken the systems of man. I am enabling you, My son. Look now and see, for I am redeemed. I'm yours this day. You are mine in every way. You have given your heart. Now I give you My best. I give you My best, says the Lord.

Brother Curry, as she was singing, I saw the Lord dancing over you. The Spirit of the Lord was dancing and as the inflection changed so did the dance, the dance of war, the dance of love, the dance of peace, the hope for the future. The Lord says, just as I have searched and looked and looked and looked and found you, I am also jealous for you, says the Lord. You are not even jealous for yourself with other ministries, and the competition thing has not taken root in your heart. And I am pleased with your heart and how you have kept the garden of your heart and the garden with the weeds being torn out so the weeds do not go down into any kind of bitterness or infection within, says the Lord.

The Lord says, son, I am going to be taking you to what it looks like to you, *"God, is this necessary?"* Don't argue with Me, son, I am giving you that land that is prime where people will say oh no, this just can't be. This is too prime a piece of land for people to build a house on. You built My house and I will build your house. The plans are going to be there. There is going to be a donor who will be available with a huge, huge amount and it will be timely given to you and you are going to know what to do with it.

The Lord says not only will it be a home but there will be provision for that training center. The Lord says you go to people, now I am bringing them to you. You have been free to give out that which I have given to you and I am giving you more. You can't even imagine the depths, the mysteries, and the **keys** that are going to be coming to you.

The Lord says, I have found you faithful. Now I will be faithful to you, and that provision there to take care of that mom and dad as the years go on, son, I will take care of them and your hands will be full of plenty of that provision to take care of them. Because the Lord says you have honored and now I will honor that and I will take care of them and they will lack for nothing.

I will bring the entire family and they will have a peace that will enable because I will give them sharpening tools. I am taking the scales off the eyes of some. There will be greater vision and acuity, and you will be surprised. Yes, you will marvel because you thought, *can this happen?* And the Lord will say, you bet.

This season is good. This season is fast. This season is for the future. You will see this season is for the very thing that I have placed in your heart. It is bigger, it is more, because you just can't see it all. It is here, says the Lord.

Doctors are going to begin to come and ask how to cure a specific disease or illness because they have heard of your reputation as a doctor and that all these people are healed. As they come and ask you how would you treat or cure this, God will give you the medical terminology that will surprise you because you aren't familiar with the words. They will sense or feel that you have the information and as they are open to receive it, you will say, now let me show you a better way, and you are going to bring many of the medical profession into the kingdom of God as you do that.

My son, even as you set your feet on this property I began to do a deepening work in the midst of your heart, and I am doing an enlarging work in the midst of your spirit. You have deposited a thing here because it is the earnest of the multiplication getting ready to happen. For surely you have come into the prophets, and even this day you are receiving the mantle of prophet and you will prophesy more than you thought was possible and you will have dreams and visions that are going to begin to open up to you. There will be third heaven revelations like John the Revelator. I will cause you to be caught away, and measures of My spirit that are even unfathomable in your mind that you thought could be possible.

For this is the season that I am opening up the gate of divine revelation and you will see a release of My Spirit to show Himself to you in a way that you have not seen. I am opening your eyes. I am opening up your heart and I am opening up your spirit, and this day, My divine deposit is going within.

Now even as you put the seed in the ground and there has been a measure of dying for you through not only to get here but to process what had to happen here, the platform of the prophets was a springboard. When you get to the platform you will see that this is a countdown . . . 10, 9, 8, 7, 6, 5, 4, 3, 2, 1 blastoff. For surely as it is established in My Word I tell My secrets to My prophets. I tell you now that which I tell you secretly, that which I read to you secretly, that which has been behind closed doors and hidden for a season will burst open and reveal by My Spirit, and you will see a worldwide impact.

You have stepped into a worldwide thrust of My Spirit going forth sent by the prophets even unto the nations. You will begin to release a demonstration of My Spirit that is beyond your imagination.

Son, I am partnering with you in this hour because the last days are coming quickly. I am calling My bride forth and I am preparing My warriors in this hour. I am going to put a trumpet to your mouth. For surely within the midst of you I have put an Amos 7 plumb line. I have put within the midst of you a line of demarcation. I have put within the midst of you My Spirit of truth. Now it will come out with forcefulness.

You will be in the situation where you will speak words that will come out of your spirit that you will want to put back in your mouth. The Lords says don't hinder the process of what I am going to do in this hour through you. I am going to cause you to be a man who will articulate in a way that will astound you. For surely the command of the English language, the pearls and poetic ability that comes out of your mouth, even to you will be a shock.

I am going to show you signs of wonders of My love. I am going to show you signs and wonders of My heart. I am going to show you signs and wonders of My portion. I spoke to you and said I would give to you some hidden mysteries; there has been some measure of that come forth within the midst of your life. This has not been the fullness. There is getting ready to open up to you an open heaven revelation that will reveal to you the armies of My heavenly realms. I am going to show you My battle strategies and plans. I am going to give you as it were CIA secret information that will reveal what I am going to be doing. Son, you will go forth establishing a thing where your foot will trod; there will I establish My kingdom.

Son, this thing will be bigger, broader, stronger, higher, and greater than you can possibly think in your mind, for this is My heart; not just for you, but My heart through you and to others. I am going to bring round about you people of divine revelation, those who are rising up as apostolic prophetic authority in this hour and you are going to link arms. There will be a gathering of eagles.

There will be a rising up of My divine last days Ark of the Covenant and there will be a shouldering of the priesthood that will come underneath the Ark of the Covenant. You will begin to demonstrate some wonders of the fulfillment of My divine plan that was established in the Old Testament and fulfilled in the New Testament, and it is the heart cry of the proclaiming of the soon coming King.

There is coming a royalty upon your head and shoulders. I am clothing you and you have no idea what the garment looks like. Son, as I begin to reveal the demonstration of this to your spirit, you will begin to weep and cry at the glory of My mighty mysteries. For surely you have no idea what My heaven and My kingdom in fullness is like.

I am getting ready to pull back the veil. I am getting ready to pull back the eyes. I am getting ready to show you some things that you have cried out for. You will see this is the thrusting of the wings of the eagle that will begin to spread and being to soar with heights in Me. You will demonstrate that ability of discernment that you have been asking for. It will settle and rise in your heart and spirit like it has not happened before.

This is a day and the hour that I am standing up in the midst of My throne. I have told you that I am sending you on a journey. I called you mighty warrior. I am raising you up as a general. I am also telling you right now the power that I have in the midst of Me to establish, to dethrone and enthrone, to release and to bind, to establish new developmental orders of government and tear down old forms of government is being put in your hand. A sickle is being put in your right hand.

There is going to come visitations to you personally. Things that I am going to do that are private experiences between you and Me. There will come the appearance of angels. There will come the revelation of seeing Me. There will come the revelation of seeing the divine order of seeing heaven. There will be moments when you will feel like saying, "Oh, God, this is so majestic, so beautiful and so huge; I don't want to stay here anymore."

The Lord says, son I have a work for you to do. I have a commission that is being placed upon you. I have a release that is coming forth out of the midst of you. There will be a joining of family. There will be a joining of teams. There will be a networking of people round about you. For surely it is time to expand the tent pegs. It is time to enlarge the tent and to establish the fullness of it. This is the hour in which I am raising up My eternal government. I am releasing to men and women the mantle, the scepter, and the authority in this hour to establish My kingdom in the midst of the hurling of hell itself.

Now, son, I am causing you to come to a place of full stature. To stand up tall and straight as an ambassador of royalty for Me. For even as you come to the house of prophets, you will leave this place with My cornerstone put in place in your spirit. I have set the foundation. I am getting ready to ramp up the beams and build the building. For it is an appointed time and season and a time to cross over and move through the gate.

I am releasing a new dispensation to your children and your wife and to those close to you. There is coming a fast change and a ripping of the wineskins that the second and third party revelation has had a measure of fire and difficulty to it. I am releasing an enabling of adjusting and grace that is supernatural. There will be a visitation that will draw you together for the purposes of My ordained eternal destiny for all of you that will cause you to flow in harmony with divine orchestration, releasing a new song.

For this is the hour, son, for you to rise and proclaim; this is the hour for you to rise and declare. It is the hour for you to set in order and to position, for surely have I placed upon you the apostolic authority of the last days prophet apostle.

I am releasing inside of your heart. I am releasing within you right now a supernatural divine network, because My hand is releasing you to a place of demonstration that I might be able to rise up in My throne. For I am standing now, says God. For I am with you and I have put My mind in you. I have placed My purposes in your heart. And you shall accomplish My will.

You will lead this last days army into battle, into victory. Your time is now at hand.

You will continue to travel but you shall travel from a base. The Training Center shall be your launching place. You will produce those who will also be mighty warriors.

You must not fear. You must not back off. You must move forward. You must attack, attack, attack. There will come a burst as it were of writing, and the books you produce will change dead traditional Christianity into a living, practical lifestyle that will produce victory.

Prophetic Word to Curry Blake Through Bill Hamon

The Lord says, son, you have cried out to Me for years. You laid out upon your side and you laid upon your belly. You waited before Me in prayer and fasting and cried out to Me. You read the heroes of faith. You read about other great men and women of God and you waited on God. And you thought: God, did I inherit that? Did I receive of that? Lord, did I partake of that? Where is the God of yesteryear? Where is the God that worked the miracles in the forties and fifties? Where is the God that worked miracles here and there? You cried out, "Oh, God!" unto the I am that I am. You felt like Moses, **forty years in the wilderness,** but finally you met the burning bush and He spoke to you. The voice of the Lord came and said do this and do that, arise and go and be and fulfill. Don't try to earn it this way. Receive it, activate it, and come forth in it. Teach My people and demonstrate, and show and teach My people that they can do the same.

The Lord says, son, I have made a new revelation to you of Mark 16. You are going to raise up believers, demonstrators of the supernatural, demonstrators of the revelation of God.

Son, get ready, you are going to expand your ministry. You are going to expand your activity. I am going to broaden your base. I am going to broaden your activity. I have opened up whole new arenas, whole new realms of nations and peoples and kinds of peoples and different kinds of peoples. You are going to affect Fundamentalists, Pentecostals, Charismatics, Prophetic, Apostolic. You are going to start reaching out and touching people. They are going to try to promote you to great arenas and great stadium meetings and you will have a few of those but you aren't going to get stuck in them.

You will have meetings where you can give out the anointing and reproduce yourself. You will have special intensified training programs where you will go out to them and bring them in. You will have intensified teaching and activating, mentoring and maturing, until you can reproduce that anointing because it is not exclusively for you, says the Lord. I have given it to you so that you can reproduce and to bring revelation and activation to My people. There will be promoters come around that will try to treat you as they did William Branham and Kathryn Kuhlman and make a big name for you and make you a big success. Already some have approached you saying, look what I can do for you. I can promote you. I can make you a big success. There will be another approaching you, saying. I can bring all this money in. I can get you on television. I can give you fame and name, but your spirit will say no, no, I want to raise up the saints. I am not the mighty one. I am not the only one. I want to convince the ministries that they can do it too. I want to see God's glory fill the earth as the waters cover the sea. I want every preacher and saint manifesting the glory.

The Lord says, you have My mind. You have My heart. You have My destiny. You have My Spirit. Now I am going to join you with those of like faith and vision and like spirit. I am going to connect you with those of like spirit. One can put a thousand to flight and two can put ten thousand to flight. Five can put a hundred and a hundred can put ten thousand.

Son, get ready. You felt alone for quite a while. You felt segregated and an oddball that nobody else has the same drive. You almost went through the Elijah syndrome. I alone am left to have the determination, the craving and desire. But the Lord says there are seven thousand out there who haven't bowed their knee to the old religious system. They have died to the old religious system and haven't died to the determination to see the glory of the Lord fill the earth.

Son, this is your day. This is your hour. I am bringing you forth, not to glorify yourself, not to glorify your name, not to glorify your position, but to glorify My power. Your name will become known. Your position will increase and your fame will spread abroad, not because you have made it happen or because you wanted it to happen, but because I did it for My name and for My glory and for My people. You will never take the gold or the glory or look for the girls. You will look for the goodness of the Lord and the glory of God and you will come forth in My power.

For the Lord says you have let Me sanctify you wholly and you let Me bring you forth. You are going to be My prophet apostle to the nations, to My people and to My Church.

The Lord says, son, this is the day and the hour that the finances, the resources, and the contacts are coming together. You are coming out of the wilderness and have crossed over Canaan land, you are crossing over Jordan, and you are ready to possess and demonstrate and bring forth, for this is the day and the hour that you have made preparation for.

For the Lord says, son, surely you will have the multitudes that you will minister to. But I have called you to be a man of God to stand when everybody else around you would run, and look into the situation, but you will take the step inward. I am going to send you some Josiahs. I am going to raise up a Josiah to be round about you. You have a heart for the young and those the world has disqualified and said this is the x generation. But the Spirit of the Lord says oh, mighty man of God, this is the hour to bring the Josiahs into the anointing. As you lay hands upon them and impart to them I will even fill the stadium with the Josiahs.

Years ago, you said there are ministries going here and going there but I don't care if I go anywhere, just let me touch the hearts of the people. The Spirit of the Lord said, you learned through the years that if you preach to the heads, you are going to get heads. If you preach to the hearts, you will get hearts. If you preach to the spirit, you will get their spirits, says the Lord. The Lord says you will touch all three, not just one. Oh, mighty man of God, surely there is coming the financial breakthrough.

I heard the Lord say, "As you have watched the system of Saul and you have observed what takes place in those courts there has been a turning in your own heart, saying, I won't do it that way, touch it that way." The Lord says, "Now is the time that I have set your face like flint.

Now is the time that I have caused your heart to be fully persuaded in your calling and destiny and the scope of your ministry. Now as you come into the place of reigning it will be a time to put on that royalty, a time to put on that mind-set, and to call for those who help and those who serve, to call for those, and put an expectancy and an expectation. For the Lord says you will do it with a righteous heart in My glory and in My favor and there will be a tightness about you.

Fear not, for it is the time to put a demand on servanthood. It is the time to call those into the position to assist that your ministry might grow to the next dimension and grow to the next magnitude. For, son, I have made your heart right in these things and you have observed what not to do. You will not manipulate. You will not use the system of Saul. Son, it is time to rise up and take on that royalty and that administrative mind-set, for surely these are the days of wisdom that you might know how to break out on the left and to break out on the right and to inherit all that I have called you to be and do.

Prophetic Word Spoken by Simeon Stewart to Curry Blake

(Simeon Stewart was ordained under A. A. Allen and was highly recognized as a prophet.)

Lord, we thank you for this thy servant, which you are using in this day and hour. We praise you because you have sent him our way—and now, Lord, lay thy hand on him in a greater measure than ever before, and in the power of the Holy Ghost rule over everything that's a weakness in him, that he become strong in the Lord and in the power of His might, for the glory of the kingdom, of the kingdom of God. Let thy word flow out of him like a river—let thy power flow through him for the glory of God, and rest upon him from this day forth in a greater measure than ever before. We thank you for it, we believe you for it.

Yea, my son, thou shall go forth in a greater measure than ever before, and thou shall see greater results, and thou shall glorify Me, for I have sent thee this way—and now, arise and shine, and let the glory of the Lord be seen upon thee, for he has come to lift thee to a new stratosphere of life, and to a new level of Me, in the name of the Lord Jesus Christ and to the glory of the Father. We thank thee for the victory now, for thy word, Lord, is a strong tower—glorify your son by the power of the Holy Ghost. Set him free in every respect until thou art glorified in all his ministry in a greater measure—we praise you for it in Jesus' name—we thank you for it, we praise You for it.

Yea, thou shalt see greater things, and thou shalt see greater days, and thou shalt have greater meetings, and behold, I am going before thee and making the crooked places straight that thou mayest walk in the pathway of Jesus, in His footsteps. Yea, thou hast come even as God's son, and now thou art sending him forth, and thou art enduing him with a greater measure of power, of understanding, of love, and Thou art using him, and thou shalt continue, in a measure that he has not known before. This is your day, this is the day of the Lord, and He has come to set you free in every aspect of Me, for the glory of His name. Thank you for it, Lord. Thank you for it, Lord. Nothing shall be too hard for you, nothing shall be impossible., I am a living God, living in you, and doing the work, and the Father shall reign, seated upon the throne of your heart, and releasing the Godhead, bodily strength to the people, for thou hast been chosen of Me and called and sent forth, and now it is time to release out of thee into all those that thou dost minister unto, for I have sent thee, and know that thou art being sent by the Holy Ghost, and by the Son, and by the Father, in Jesus' Name.

Prophetic Word Given Through Simeon Stewart To Curry R. Blake

Thou shall go forth in a greater measure than ever before and thou shall see greater results. Thou shalt glorify Me. For I have sent thee this way. Now arise and shine and let the glory of the Lord be seen upon thee. For He has come to lift thee into a new stratosphere of life, into a new level of being. Thou shalt see greater things. Thou shaltl see greater days. Thou shalt see greater meetings. I am going before thee and making crooked places straight that thou mayest walk in the pathway of Jesus in His footsteps.

Thou hast come as God's Son came and now, Lord, Thou art sending him forth and enduing him with a greater measure of power, and continue in a measure that thou has not known before. This is your day and He has come to set you free in every aspect of Me. Nothing shall be too hard for you. Nothing shall be impossible. The living God living in you is doing the work. The Father, along with you, is seated upon the throne of your heart. I release into you the bodily strength of the Godhead, for thou has been chosen of Me and called and sent forth and now it is pouring out of thee into all those that thou must minister unto for I have sent thee and know that thou art being sent by the Holy Ghost and by the Son and by the Father.

Heaven has come down today and visited this place and He is coming down in a greater measure. This is the Word of the Lord to you today, thou shall be stronger in all thy dealings with other people and the faith of the Father, the Son, and the Holy Ghost combined shall do the work unto you and your word of authority shall not be questioned, because I am standing behind My Word to bring it to pass, saith the Lord

Thou art yet to see greater things. I am pushing the powers of darkness back. I am holding them at bay that the work of the Lord will go forward. This is My hour to work. This is My day. I am coming in power like you have never seen before to work the works that I worked when I was upon earth. Greater works of these that I do shall you do also because I go to the Father. The Comforter could not come until I went away and now He is here and the three of you in Him combined. I shall turn the world as it were upside down and break the bands asunder.

The doors that were closed shall begin to be opened and the Word of God will be opened like never before. This is My choice. This is the day that I will begin to work through you, My son, My child. I love you with an everlasting love. I will continue to use you and bless you as you have never been blessed and used before.

This is what God is going to do, what He is doing, and what He is going to bring forth. He is going to spring forth speedily because the days are short and time is short. He is coming forth in a greater measure. He is coming into you in a new measure. He is going to break those bands and loose those strings that have held you back, and now the windows of heaven are open over you and thou shall go. Greater is God in you than he that is in the world, for the glory of His name.

Go forth unto the ends of the earth, for the doors are being opened and you shall prosper. Your ministry will be greater. You will stand where others have not stood and you shall speak words that have not been spoken before because it was not My time. Now it is time to arise and shake yourself. I am sending you under the canopy of my divine blessings and thou shalt not fail. Thou shalt be stronger in every measure until you glorify Me in the earth and bring forth everything according to My will.

Go in My strength. Go in My power. Go forth in My Word and thou shalt not fail because it can't fail. My Word has never failed. I brought forth the earth and hung it on nothing. I brought forth the stars, the sun, and the moon, and everything, and they were made by the Words of My mouth. And when thou doest speak, My Word will go through thy mouth like the fire and the created sword it will cleave asunder and bring to pass the will of God in every life you pray for. I am God and there is no one else beside Me.

The Word of the Lord declares it and it shall come to pass and you shall not faint nor fail because my strength within you is holding you up and making you strong and giving you understanding. And words you have not spoken shall pour out of your mouth, the revelation knowledge of God that's been hidden from ages and now in these last days is coming to pass. I am declaring and sending it forth and you have manna that has been hidden and now it is being uncovered. Now you will unfold the Word as never before because God is in it.

This is God's time to work and to bring it forth and to speak in no uncertain tones. For I am declaring unto you that My word is a strong tower and it is birthed in Jesus the Rock and the stony hearted and is causing them to humble themselves under the mighty hand of God. Churches are going to be turned about face because your ministry and because of your obedience and pastors are going to come to the knowledge of the truth because of your ministry for the glory of God. You shall see results and it shall come to pass, for God's Word is true. It cannot fail, and neither will you fail. His hand is on you.

Thou art being made stronger because of My Word. The Word of God, His timing is ready to be ministered by the power of the Holy Ghost such as you have never ministered before, for thou hast been given intelligence from the mind of the Father, the Son, and the Holy Ghost. He is the director general of all the activities of the Father and Son and He is greater in you today than ever before. Go in the strength of the Word of the Lord and know that He, **He** is still to all as you have never seen heard or understood. And He is with you.

God is releasing potential that has never been touched by mankind. He Himself is opening doors of divine strength and purity, love, salvation, and of healing and miracles, signs and wonders that have never been seen by man. He is opening the door over you of His ministry of miracles, unprecedented by any of His chosen ones on the face of the earth today.

Thou has strength that is coming from Me, says the Lord, and it is coming from Me and it will continue to flow to the ends of the earth. In me it is overflowing. It cannot be stopped. It will continue to flow and flow over and wash away the sickness and sins and everything that Satan has put upon the body of Jesus Christ. He is throwing off the shackles and sending His angels to minister, and all the ministering spirits sent to minister unto those that are the heirs of salvation.

You are an heir and a joint heir of Jesus Christ. All that He has spoken shall come to pass. It can't be turned aside or stopped. It is an overflowing stream that has no end. Believe me. Just believe my faith is working in thee and the faith of the Son of God who has brought all things into being by His Word and now His Word is going to bring all things into submission unto Himself through thee, and because you are going to speak My Word that created all things, the same word is restoring My people and bringing you up in a level that you have never known.

Now is my time, arise in the strength of the Lord and go in the strength of His power and know that thou hast been in a singular matter today. The Word of the Lord is cleaving unto thee. All of thy being is being penetrated by the living Word of God until thou art nothing but a walking epistle known and read of all men, used by and for the glory of God. Knowing all things, thy understanding is being opened into the full mouth of the hidden manna that has not been distributed to the body. You are going to feed my sheep and my lambs as they have not been fed on the heavenly manna, and the dew of heaven is resting upon your soul. The achievement of all the word of the Lord has been declared unto you. It shall stand, says the Lord.

Drink again of the fountains that shall never run dry. Drink of that fountain of life and the water of life that is flowing through thee. The bread of life is being ministered to thee. My sheep are crying out. They are holding out their hands for help. Thou art going to put meat on their table and flesh on their bones, the spiritual flesh of the Lord itself and not the carnal minds. He is driving it back and holding it at bay that the word of God may prosper continuously. There will be no end to what God will show you and make you to speak and cause you to bring forth for He saith it, says the Lord.

The Lord is speaking to us from heaven above out of our souls, our hearts, our spirits, and our minds. He is speaking out from the depths of our being. The very depths of the Lord Jesus Christ is in us. He is declaring what He wants to do. He is releasing the bonds and the pressure and taking away the difficulty in the human life and the body of Christ. He is moving, He is building a wall of fire round about them. He is causing the grace of God to be seen as it has never been seen before, such as it was in the early Church, great grace was upon them all. Grace is coming in power into the Body of Christ and into the lives of the people and His ministers. The faith was once delivered unto the saints that faith is taking hold of them now because they have contended for it and it is coming and it is in your heart. You are going to experience it and see it. Oh, the wonders of His love, His grace and His power.

You cannot limit Him. He cannot be limited. You can't stop it. He is in you and working. He is going to continue to work until his name is known from coast to coast and around the world. He is going to continue to pour out his spirit, for this is my days, saith the Lord, that I have spoken by my holy prophets and apostles in times past and it is here. It is upon you. You have the touch of the apostolic ministry working in you.

The confirmation of all that I have spoken shall come to pass because of apostolic authority. It shall stay in you and you shall speak it forth and declare and manifest it and you shall see the glory of the Lord. Your face is going to shine with His glory. And others shall know the Christ is in His servant and came forth in you in new life a new understanding. This is your day, son. This is your day with the Lord. He is going to send you forth. This is it. This is the time.

You can't out-dress the Lord. He knows the deep cry of your heart. He knows the longing of your soul. He knows all about the innermost secrets of your being and He is strengthening them and they are coming to pass. They will be greater than you realize. You are going to see the hand of God as you have never seen it before. This is My day to work with you, My son. I have said before, as it is with Christ Jesus, so shall it be in thee. That power outdoing all the past, all thy word, and all thy promises.

They that wait upon the Lord shall renew their strength. They shall mount up with wings of eagles. They shall run and not be weary. They shall walk and not faint. This is your day to run. Take the message and run with it. This is your day. The door is open. You are being strengthened. The door is open. It is being enlarged. Your field of service is opening up in a newer measure as never before. You are going forth into fields untouched by the power of God and you are going to see great things, for this is My day. I have many sons and I am preparing them unto glory. I am anointing those that I am putting on the field and sending forth. It is Christ in you that is bringing it forth. It is His plan and it is His purpose. The light that shines unto thee, even unto the West, so shall also the coming of the Son of Man be in revelation and understanding knowledge, in power and healing and miracles and signs and wonders to no end. For thou has begun and He is going to finish. The work that He has begun in you shall be made strong and last until the end of the time, for thou are strong in the Lord and in the power of His might. You will go forth with the Word as you have never spoken before by revelation.

We can't imagine what God wants to do but He is telling us. He is declaring it unto us. He is making it plain. He is opening the books upon high of all My people and all My commandments, all My sayings, all My Scriptures, all My teachings are upon all the hearts and minds written by the finger of God. I am opening as it were the library of the foundation truth, and bringing it forth in a measure that has never been taught, because I am the teacher. I am the beginning and the end. I am the first and the last and there is no one else beside Me.

There is a fountain in the house of David and He is opening that well, causing salvation to flow because Jesus sets on the throne of David in your heart. He is ministering life and health, understanding. He is reigning in life through you and through His servants. He is reigning.

Open your soul in a measure that you have never known. Now you are accepted. You have opened your heart, you have opened your life, and go forth in a strength that has never been known. It has come and it is going to stay and remain and become more forceful to you, and all thy endeavors shall come to an end and shall be through Me, says the Lord, through the power of My might as it is My power backing thee up and has made all things, and you will become as it were a shining hand like thou has never been before, perfect in thy being, thy understanding, and thy waiting upon for the glory that is on its way. It's on its way.

Jesus said I am the way the truth and the life, walk in Me and thou shall not stumble and thou shall have the best as your understanding. Turn thee aside, for My power is doing the work, his power, the power of the Holy One of Israel. The power of the Holy Ghost. You are going to be a new man in Christ Jesus the Lord.

One thing you have desired is more miracles in your ministry. He has been talking to you about it. He is going to confirm your call and grant you the liberty to believe that you will have a ministry of miracles and not be satisfied until you do. Press in, the Lord is with you on this. He is searching your heart. He knows your intentions in the future. He knows all those things. Let Him make your plans and He will direct you and guide you in a fuller ministry than you have ever known. He is with you right now to show you the way to speak words of comfort and understanding to your heart and to make you trust and obey. The Word of God is with you and in you. The whole book is there in you, written on the tables of your heart. The Holy Ghost is with you because the kingdom of God is in you. This does not come by observation, Jesus said. The Father, the Son, and the Holy Ghost all are in the kingdom and in your heart.

Prophetic Word Given Through Simeon Stewart To Curry R. Blake

God bless you, my brother. There are many things that should make you grow and will make your ministry expand more than it has in the past with the blessing of the Lord. You can't miss it because it is a great promise of God that is ours. Christ Jesus is coming soon, brother, and He wants to get the church ready. He has supplied additional gifts to the Church and the Body of Christ to make it possible for the Church to be ready when He comes. So commit these ways and your ways and the power unto Him and know He is going to grant you all that He has.

My son, I say unto thee I am your benefactor. I am your Lord. I am your God, and I am making plans for your future. To your amazement they will be coming, as you are faithful to Me and My Word. I will show you the way and you will do great things under the mighty power of the Holy Ghost, nothing short of glory. Therefore look up and trust, for God is your helper He stands by you through thick and thin. Regardless of what is out there He will open the doors and make the way. He is your leader and He is your guide. He will lead you into eternal blessing. God is your helper right now. He is helping you press into the presence to gain full fellowship with Him and all that which He has for you in the future.

God will give you everything that you stand in need of. He is the all-powerful One. This is His work, and naturally He is interested in you. He is going to bless you in a greater measure than ever before and you will be amazed at what He will help you do. You have had miracles in your heart and He is satisfying the longing of your heart because He searches the heart. He knows your frame. He knows what you think of. He will be with you all the way. You can't be discouraged because God is with you. He is with you always. The Triune God is with you always.

John G. Lake Ministries

A: The International Divine Healing Association

The International Divine Healing Association (IDHA) is, as its name implies, an international association of Christian believers that practice and teach divine healing. Membership is open to anyone who professes Christ as Lord and believes that God still heals.

Many varying beliefs are represented, but all have the common denominator of believing in Christ as Lord and Savior. The IDHA has annual and seasonal conferences, as well as mans to help promote the ministries of its membership.

The IDHA is also involved in helping publish books on divine healing by its members and publish articles written by members in its magazine, as well as list its members on the IDHA website.

For more information, contact us at: contact@jglm.org

B: The International Apostolic Council

The International Apostolic Council is the association of ministries and ministers who have been trained and/or ordained or licensed and certified by John G. Lake Ministries.

The IAC now has associates all over the world. By becoming a member of the IAC, you will have access to mentors, coaches, and trainers that will help you walk out the truths taught by JGLM. You will also receive regular updates in training and attendance at specialized training events.

You will receive newsletters, magazines, have access to online videos, webinars, and podcasts, as well as access to archived materials. The IAC will also help members with placement in ministry internship programs and mission trips around the world.

For more information, contact us at iac@jglm.org

C: Ordination and/or Licensing

Licensing and ordination are available through the Credentialing Department. A course of ministerial studies is required, along with evaluations and recommendations by JGLM leaders.

For more information, contact us at: iac@jglm.org

D: Church Planting

JGLM is committed to planting churches around the world. We are training missionaries and church planting teams through Dominion Bible Institute.

For more information contact us at: iac@jglm.org

E: LifeTeams

What Are LifeTeams?

JGLM LifeTeams are small groups of believers who desire to grow and function efficiently in their Christian walk.

The purpose of JGLM LifeTeams is to reach their cities for Christ and to grow believers into mature sons and daughters of God. JGLM LifeTeams are often the beginning steps toward planting a JGLM church.

For more information, contact us atlifeteams@jglm.org

How Do LifeTeams Operate?

JGLM Life Teams are similar to cell groups and/or G-12 Groups. There are specific JGLM Life Team training materials, as well as a JGLM Life Team Forum to help the team grow properly.

How Do I Start A Life Team?

Simply contact us at lifeteams@jglm.org

We will be glad to get you started. We can also direct you to an existing Life Team and/or put you in contact with other JGLMers in your area.

F: Divine Healing Institute

The Divine Healing Institute (DHI) is the divine healing training and research arm of JGLM and was founded by John G. Lake in 1914, making it the oldest divine healing training school in existence.

1. The DHI is responsible for the actual certification and ongoing training of Divine Healing Technicians.

2. Divine Healing Technician Training Seminars are conducted under the auspices of the DHI, as well as the training and certification of DHT Trainers.

3. JGLM Healing Rooms are operated under the direction of the DHI.

All applications for operating a JGLM-sanctioned Healing Room and the training of JGLM Healing Rooms personnel is conducted by the DHI.

For more information, contact us at:
dhidirector@jglm.org

G: IABC/JGLSoM—Dominion Bible Institute

The Educational and Ministerial Training arm of JGLM is carried out through the International Apostolic Bible College (IABC), the John G. Lake School of Ministry (JGLSoM), and Dominion Bible Institute (DBI).

1. International Apostolic Bible College (IABC)
The IABC is the residential Bible College operated by JGLM.

2. John G. Lake School of Ministry (JGLSoM)
The JGLSoM is the Correspondence Bible School operated by JGLM.

3. Dominion Bible Institute (DBI)
Dominion Bible Institute is the online, distance learning Bible Institute operated by JGLM.

For more information on any of the above, contact us at: dbiaccounts@jglm.org

H: Dominion Life Movement

The Dominion Life Movement is the sum total of all activities of JGLM trained ministers and affiliates. The purpose of the Dominion Life Movement is to bring the total Gospel to every creature throughout the earth. The Dominion Life Movement is being propagated through every possible means of communication and training. It's not just a name, it is living the Gospel of Jesus Christ through every situation, overcoming every obstacle, achieving victory in every trial, thereby bringing glory to God through an overcoming, victorious faith that exemplifies the dominion God originally commanded man to walk in.

J: JGLM Partner Program

Newsletter - Partners of JGLM will receive a free monthly newsletter that will detail the ministry's upcoming activities. Each newsletter will also have partner specials.

Partner Only Meetings—Partner Only Meetings will be held in conjunction with Divine Healing Technician

Training Schools being held around the country. Normally, the POM will be held the day before a DHTTS starts. POM will be a time of fellowship and personal ministry.

CD of The Month—Each partner will receive a free CD or DVD each month that is specially picked out for partners only.

Partners are very important to JGLM. Our partners enable us to give our material to those who cannot afford it (prisons and missions).

Partners are also our main line of prayer support

You are left unsatisfied by the status quo...
You know you were meant to be a participant and not just a spectator...
You ask "Why not?..." more than "Why?"...
You believe that today can be better than yesterday...
You know you were meant to walk among the Giants of the Faith, and you want the tools & training that can make it happen...
When you hear the exploits of God's Generals, you can picture yourself doing them...

If this describes you, then you ARE JGLM... whether you know it or not.

COME.
LET'S CHANGE THE WORLD.

 John G. Lake Ministries
SAME MESSAGE. SAME POWER. SAME RESULTS.

LIFE TEAM
The Saints Army
lifeteams@jglm.org

Go out into all the world. Preach the gospel, heal the sick, cast out demons and make disciples

The Teaching That Birthed A Legend Is Now Raising An Army.

Get Yours Today
Call **888-293-6591**
or Visit Us Online
store.jglm.org

John G. Lake Ministries
SAME MESSAGE. SAME POWER. SAME RESULTS.

Glory to God, Freedom for All!

Join us online every Sunday at 10am:
broadcast.jglm.org
To learn more about Dominion Life visit:
jglm.org/dominion-life-church
or email: dliac@jglm.org

Church Membership Requirements

1. Must confess Jesus as Lord and that you are saved and born again.

2. Must at least be seeking and expecting to be filled with the Holy Spirit in accordance with Acts Chapter 2 (speaking with other tongues).

3. Must agree with the JGLM/IAC Statement of Faith, obtained by emailing us at: dliac@jglm.org.

4. You agree to pray for us according to the prayer directives that we will send to all church members on a regular basis.

5. You agree to support the church through tithes and offerings. Tithes and offerings must be sent to the church address and MUST be noted as Tithes/Offerings.

6. You agree to work towards becoming a certified DHT. Our hope is that ALL DLIAC members work toward becoming a certified DHT to advance the kingdom through this body. For information on becoming a DHT contact us by email at: iac@jglm.org or you can find all information on our website at www.jglm.org.

7. You agree to remain in the unity of the Spirit by living a life in accordance with the constitution and bylaws of the I.A.C.